$19,95

D0007661

Black Americans in North Carolina
and the South

Black Americans in North Carolina and the South

Edited by Jeffrey J. Crow and Flora J. Hatley

The University of North Carolina Press

Chapel Hill and London

Library of Congress Cataloging in Publication Data
Main entry under title:

Black Americans in North Carolina and the South.

   1. Afro-Americans—North Carolina—History—
Addresses, essays, lectures. 2. Afro-Americans—
Southern States—History—Addresses, essays, lectures.
3. North Carolina—History—Addresses, essays, lectures.
4. Southern States—History—Addresses, essays,
lectures. I. Crow, Jeffrey J. II. Hatley, Flora J.
E185.93.N6E87   1984   975'.00496073   83-21762
ISBN 0-8078-1593-4

To the memory of

Frederick Douglas Alexander

(1910–1980)

and to

John Hope Franklin

Contents

Illustrations

Tables

Introduction

Since the mid-1970s the North Carolina Division of Archives and History has sponsored three symposiums on various aspects of North Carolina history in an effort to encourage new research and interpretation of the state's past. In 1975 the division, in association with the Institute of Early American History and Culture, Williamsburg, Virginia, Duke University, North Carolina State University, and the University of North Carolina at Chapel Hill, held a symposium on the experience of revolution in North Carolina and the South. Two years later the division hosted a symposium devoted to the study and writing of North Carolina history. Subsequently, the papers presented at both of these symposiums were published as *The Southern Experience in the American Revolution* and *Writing North Carolina History*.[1]

As the Division of Archives and History attempted to promote a more thorough examination of the state's history during the 1970s, it also broadened and expanded its programs of interpretation of and materials on black North Carolinians. In 1975 the North Carolina Museum of History mounted an exhibit of furniture made by Thomas Day, a noted black cabinetmaker in antebellum Caswell County, and published an accompanying catalog. The following year the division's Survey and Planning Branch undertook a preliminary investigation of significant historic structures in the state's black community. To assist black genealogists the State Archives completed the arrangement of cohabitation bonds of ex-slaves who sought to formalize their marriages immediately following the Civil War and instituted regular workshops on black genealogy. The Archives also issued a preliminary guide to black-related records. The Historical Publications Section, meanwhile, published two original studies on the state's black history. In 1978, after receiving a grant from the National Endowment for the Humanities, the North Carolina Museum of History opened a highly acclaimed exhibit titled "The Black Presence in North Carolina," which stood for a year, published an accompanying catalog, and produced a phonograph album of traditional black music, *Eight-Hand Sets & Holy Steps*.[2]

In 1979, recognizing the growing importance of this aspect of the division's mission, the North Carolina General Assembly appropriated funds to establish an ongoing black history program and designated the second week of each February as Black History Week in North Carolina. The first coordinator for this black history program was Donna Bonita Herring, who has been succeeded by Flora J. Hatley. Also in 1979, under the guidance of William S. Price, Jr., now director of the Division of Archives and History, planning began for a major symposium titled "The History of Black Americans in North Carolina and the South." This symposium met in February 1981 and assembled some of the leading scholars in the field of black history. The papers presented at that symposium have been revised and edited for inclusion in this book.

Despite being specialists in the field of Afro-American history, the contributing scholars faced formidable obstacles in preparing their essays. Traditionally, North Carolina's black heritage has received little study. An occasional book or article on black Carolinians has entered the state's historical canon, but only a few historians have devoted extensive research to the black experience in North Carolina. When Tar Heel blacks have appeared in historical studies, more often than not they have been portrayed in the context of race relations, as unnamed, passive victims of racial prejudice, or as troublesome aberrations in the social and political order. Slavery, for example, has attracted several interpreters; historians have been quick to point to North Carolina, with its relatively fewer slaves and fewer large slaveholders, as a notable exception to southern norms, but they have given little attention to the black infrastructure or the impact of slavery on the state's social and economic life. The political dissent and debate surrounding slavery in North Carolina, from the Quakers to Hinton R. Helper to ad valorem taxation, have captured historians' interest, but few scholars have examined black Carolinians with the same intensity. For too many years the legal apparatus binding slaves and its alleged benevolent amelioration preoccupied North Carolina historians, who thus failed to measure just what life was like for slaves forced to live under such conditions.[3] The understanding of slavery in nineteenth-century North Carolina has advanced little since the pioneering studies of Guion Griffis Johnson and John Hope Franklin in 1937 and 1943, respectively.[4]

No matter what area of black history in North Carolina the contributors approached, they found the same paucity of interpretive materials. In their earlier works they had shown innovation and a propensity to challenge older, more orthodox interpretations. But in preparing essays for this book each had to define a specific subject on which to concentrate, in some cases to search diligently for appropriate sources, and even to devise new methods of inquiry. Consequently, the essays published here include much original and important new research but also speculations on methodology and comparisons with other regions, colonies, and states to compensate for the yawning gaps in North Carolina's secondary literature on black history.

Raymond Gavins begins with a critical review of North Carolina's black historiography. Although he acknowledges the general dearth of published materials on Tar Heel blacks, he discloses a trove of unpublished studies. Still, the need for a broad synthesis of the state's black heritage remains the principal challenge for this generation of historians. Gavins sensitively and effectively interweaves threads of the state's history with the social, political, economic, and intellectual skeins in which studies from several disciplines have been written. His is an evolutionary interpretation of North Carolina's black history and the literature on it.

Leland Ferguson provides an interdisciplinary approach to the South's black history. One of only a handful of anthropologists who are currently studying black material culture in the South, Ferguson has few works on which to build broad interpretations or to make sweeping generalizations about the life-style of southern blacks, particularly in the eighteenth and nineteenth centuries. He posits therefore a methodological approach in which history and archaeology can uncover—literally and figuratively—new information about the Afro-American past, reinforce each other, and develop not only new lines of inquiry but new ways in which to view the cultural interplay of black, white, and red Southerners. His discovery of possible African craftsmanship in colonial pottery sherds suggests the richness of the material culture historians continue to neglect.

Marvin L. Michael Kay and Lorin Lee Cary, who are writing a full-length study of black Carolinians in the colonial period, employ ingenious methodological techniques to open a whole new range of questions and overturn several earlier assertions about the demographic characteristics of North Carolina's black and white populations in the generation before the American Revolution. Demonstrating extraordinary thoroughness and familiarity with the colony's provincial and county records, Kay and Cary give historians the first outlines of black and white servitude in the colony, patterns of population growth through both natural increase and the slave trade, the minimum demographic conditions necessary to allow a black community to take root and flourish, and other demographic information that will help remove vast areas of ignorance about black life in eighteenth-century North Carolina.

With the flowering of black history in the 1960s, fashionable white liberal biases crept into many interpretations of the nation's black experience. One of the most familiar and enduring has been the Yankee schoolmarm. Whereas earlier in the century these women were seen as enigmatic do-gooders, in an era of civil rights ferment they came to be viewed as heroines who went south during and after the Civil War for idealistic, religious, and altruistic reasons to teach and inspire the freedmen. Nearly overlooked have been the black teachers from the North who, as Linda M. Perkins carefully documents, offered their talents, skills, and dedication, but often confronted stiff-necked and unbending discrimination from white teachers and the organizations that sponsored educational efforts in the South. Perkins's findings reassess previous assumptions about northern benevolent societies, white attitudes toward teaching blacks, and contrasting responses of black pupils to white and black teachers.

Howard N. Rabinowitz, whose seminal work on urban race relations in the New South has already toppled several comfortable shibboleths about the period's "forgotten alternatives,"[5] uses his essay to explore differences in urban race relations between North and South. Rabinowitz notes that urban black history has concentrated almost exclusively on the North and thus has neglected a critical period for black Southerners in urban areas. He introduces, for instance, an original profile of the class and social status of the blacks who served on Raleigh's city council in the last decades of the nineteenth century. Though southern cities had shifted from patterns of exclusion to segregation after the Civil War, a noteworthy step in itself, according to Rabinowitz, he concludes that by the turn of the century the movement toward disfranchisement and increasingly rigid discrimination made conditions ripe for the so-called Great Migration that commenced during World War I. Northern cities, which seemed so much more attractive politically, socially, and economically in this period, however, would also undergo significant changes in treatment of, temperament toward, and opportunities for blacks after the war.

The concluding essay by Todd L. Savitt examines a topic that has received scant attention: black medical institutions. Savitt, whose previous work has established the emergence of "racial" medicine in the nineteenth-century scientific and intellectual communities,[6] discusses the unsteady rise and lamentable disappearance of black medical schools in the late nineteenth and early twentieth centuries, with particular emphasis on the Leonard Medical School at Shaw University in Raleigh. Despite a promising beginning with support from northern white philanthropy, the school never had a firm financial base on which to grow and prosper. The need for black health care in the South, though recognized as critical in the black community and in some segments of the white community, could not overcome the general indifference, if not disdain, of the medical profession toward the delivery of medical services to blacks and the training of black physicians and nurses. The resultant insufficient funding made it impossible for Leonard and other black medical schools to keep up with advances in medicine and medical instruction. Thus, as Savitt's study suggests, the growing professionalization of medicine ironically helped to perpetuate a system of neglect and to nurture institutional racism.

Collectively, these essays not only present new information and new interpretations but also chart new areas of inquiry that demand further research. Yet, given the dearth of previous analyses of North Carolina's black heritage, these essays, in conjunction with past research, simply frame the subjects, methodologies, and perspectives which, if pursued, might profitably reveal fresh insights about the history of black Americans. After almost a century of writing, the thin corpus of works on North Carolina's black history only begins to probe, much less explain, trends in black ecology, Afro-American marital and familial values and patterns during and after slavery, the central role of work on farms and increasingly in urban areas, the attempts by blacks to organize effectively as farmers and laborers, the instrumental roles of religious and fraternal orders, the matrices of life as revealed through material, literary, and oral culture, the nature and identity of black leadership, rhythms of protest and accommodation, the ways in which blacks coped with disfranchisement, segregation, depression, and even the civil rights movement in the twentieth century, and a multitude of other questions. What these essays have done, nonetheless, is to limn the richness and variety of the Afro-American experience and to invite others to share in the recovery of that past.

Jeffrey J. Crow
Flora J. Hatley

NOTES

1. Jeffrey J. Crow and Larry E. Tise, eds., *The Southern Experience in the American Revolution* (Chapel Hill: University of North Carolina Press, 1978); Jeffrey J. Crow and Larry E. Tise, eds., *Writing North Carolina History* (Chapel Hill: University of North Carolina Press, 1979).

2. Rodney Barfield, *Thomas Day, Cabinetmaker* (Raleigh: Department of Cultural Resources, 1975); Jeffrey J. Crow, *The Black Experience in Revolutionary North Carolina* (Raleigh: Department of Cultural Resources, 1977); Joe A. Mobley, *James City: A Black Community in North Carolina, 1863–1900*, Research Reports from the Division of Ar-

2

chives and History, no. 1 (Raleigh: Department of Cultural Resources, 1981); Thornton W. Mitchell, *Preliminary Guide to Records Relating to Blacks in the North Carolina State Archives*, Archives Information Circular No. 17 (Raleigh: Department of Cultural Resources, 1980); and Jeffrey J. Crow and Robert E. Winters, Jr., eds., *The Black Presence in North Carolina* (Raleigh: North Carolina Museum of History, 1978). See also Earl E. Thorpe, *The Uses of Black History* (Raleigh: Department of Cultural Resources, 1980), which was first delivered as an address commemorating Black History Week at the Division of Archives and History in February 1980.

3. See, for example, Ernest J. Clark, Jr., "Aspects of the North Carolina Slave Code, 1715–1860," *North Carolina Historical Review* 39 (Spring 1962): 148–64.

4. Guion Griffis Johnson, *Ante-Bellum North Carolina: A Social History* (Chapel Hill: University of North Carolina Press, 1937), pp. 468–612; John Hope Franklin, *The Free Negro in North Carolina, 1790–1860* (Chapel Hill: University of North Carolina Press, 1943).

5. Howard N. Rabinowitz, *Race Relations in the Urban South, 1865–1890* (New York: Oxford University Press, 1978).

6. Todd L. Savitt, *Medicine and Slavery: The Diseases and Health Care of Blacks in Antebellum Virginia* (Champaign: University of Illinois Press, 1978); see also Todd L. Savitt, "The Use of Blacks for Medical Experimentation and Demonstration in the Old South," *Journal of Southern History* 48 (August 1982): 331–48.

Black Americans in North Carolina and the South

1. A "Sin of Omission"

Black Historiography in North Carolina

Raymond Gavins

Almost a century ago, before the Wilmington riot of 1898 and the passage of the segregation statute and the grandfather clause confirmed the position of the Old North State in the mainstream of New South Negrophobia, Edward Augustus Johnson, Raleigh attorney and educator, prefaced *A School History of the Negro* thusly:

> During my experience of eleven years as a teacher, I have often felt that the children of the race ought to study some work that would give them a little information on the many brave deeds and noble characters of their own race. I have often observed the sin of omission and commission on the part of white authors, most of whom seem to have written exclusively for white children, and studiously left out the many creditable deeds of the Negro. The general tone of most of the histories taught in our schools has been that of the inferiority of the Negro, whether actually said in so many words, or left to be implied from the highest laudation of the deeds of one race to the complete exclusion of those of the other. It must, indeed, be a stimulus to any people to be able to refer to their ancestors as distinguished in deeds of valor, and peculiarly so to the colored people. But how must the little colored child feel when he has completed the assigned course in U.S. History and in it found not one word of credit, not one word of favorable comment for even one among the millions of his foreparents who have lived through nearly three centuries of his country's history![1]

These exhortations foreshadowed black studies, but neither the man nor the text is well known.

Obvious gifts for self-expression, and the courage to employ them, made E. A. Johnson a respected member of the Talented Tenth. "I was one of a family of eleven and belonged to a man who owned thirty slaves. When I was 4 years old my father and mother and my ten brothers and sisters were set free by President Lincoln's proclamation," he recalled once. "A few years later, as a young boy, I was able to study at night, and soon entered Washington School." Founded by northern missionaries, this little academy in Raleigh prepared him to enter Atlanta University, that lower South haven of freedmen's education where the humblest graduate could aspire to distinction. Richard R. Wright, for example, obtained a summer studentship at Harvard, where he consulted with historians John Fisk and Justin Winsor. Besides turning out monographs, Wright became a college president and military officer. James Weldon Johnson, noted lyricist, poet, and writer, became executive secretary of the National Association for the Advancement of Colored People. E. A. Johnson served awhile as an Atlanta principal; afterward he returned home to head the institution of his youth and to earn a bachelor of laws from Shaw University. Energetic and proud, he asked, a half century before the matter provoked debate, that teachers make sure "the word Negro is written with a capital N. It deserves to be so enlarged and will help, perhaps, to magnify the race it stands for in the minds of those who see it."[2]

The book demonstrated minimal detachment; Johnson combined pedagogy and pride. Of the few narratives on the subject then published, only one, George Washington Williams's *History of the Negro Race in America*, told the full story. Appearing in 1883, a cumbersome, two-volume tome, it proved exhaustive and exhausting. So to reach the young, an essential but slighted audience, Johnson scaled down the Williams model to classroom size and usability. His format was innovative indeed, with biographical sketches, brief calendars, crisp summaries of events, excerpts from documents, and illustrations. Several of the thirty-five short chapters covered Negro Carolinians, and all entwined themes of collective insurgency, internal development, interracial relations,

Fig. 1-1. Edward Augustus Johnson, assemblyman, author, educator, and North Carolina's pioneer advocate of Afro-American history. From Charles H. Wesley, *The International Library of Negro Life and History*, Vol. 10, *The Quest for Equality* (Washington, D.C.: The Association for the Study of Afro-American Life and History, 1968), p. 110; reprinted by permission of the ASALH.

leadership thought, and postbellum progress. "We shall rise, not by dragging others down," the closing reads, "but by encouraging those who are up to extend down to us the helping hand, which we must quickly grasp, and by its help lift ourselves up."[3]

The flame of uplift flared and then flickered more brightly, but Johnson was ignored by his native state. Soon *A School History* entered a third edition, and the schoolmaster began over a decade of tenure in Shaw's department of law, where he served alternately or simultaneously as professor and dean. In time he became a Raleigh alderman, an assistant United States attorney, chairman of the fourth district Republican party, and thrice a national convention delegate. Somehow, he also found time to write. His *History of Negro Soldiers in the Spanish-American War*, released right after the Wilmington tragedy, denounced mob rule, separation of the races, and restriction of the suffrage. "The colored people will eventually leave those places where they are maltreated," Johnson prophesied, "but 'whether it is better to suffer the ills we now bear than flee to those we know not of,' is the question." His novel, *Light Ahead for the Negro*, whose white heroine treats blacks as equals, showed nevertheless that he was still hopeful. "At the bottom of southern society there is a vein of sympathy and helpfulness for the Negro," asserted the author, "and . . . this feeling should be cultivated and nourished that it may grow stronger and finally supplant harsher sentiments." Yet reverses, personal and political, forced him by 1907 to establish residence in New York City. Elected the first black assemblyman there, determined to improve life for Harlem migrants, he championed civil rights and economic justice. When the Tar Heel expatriate died in 1944, his role as Carolina's pioneer advocate of Afro-American history had been forgotten.[4]

Growth of the Study of
Black History in North Carolina

A review of the strides toward recognition of the black contribution to the state's history between Johnson's day and ours, an

A SCHOOL HISTORY

(FOURTH READER GRADE)

OF THE

NEGRO RACE IN THE UNITED STATES.

WITH A SHORT INTRODUCTION

AS TO

THE ORIGIN OF THE RACE.

ALSO A

SHORT SKETCH OF LIBERIA.

BY

EDWARD A. JOHNSON, LL.B.,
Former Principal of the Washington School, Raleigh, N. C.

————

REVISED EDITION, 1894.
Under the Supervision of
S. M. FINGER,
Ex-State Superintendent of Public Instruction of North Carolina, Newton, N. C.
and
W. B. KENDRICK,
Raleigh, N. C.

————

RALEIGH, N. C.:
EDWARDS & BROUGHTON, PUBLISHERS.
1894.

Fig. 1-2. Title page of *A School History of the Negro Race in the United States*. Edward A. Johnson condensed his textbook from George Washington Williams's two-volume *History of the Negro Race in America* (New York: G. P. Putnam's Sons, 1883). From the files of the North Carolina Division of Archives and History, Raleigh.

appropriate introduction to this essay, can be instructive. (Such a review reveals, besides intellectual racism, that new understandings of the past frequently have resulted from efforts to change the present. Once concerned people lead, some historians follow.) For certain, the attitudes that troubled Johnson lingered. Memory of bondage, emancipation bitterness, and political violence set the ground rules. Carolinians living under Jim Crow education, employment, and enfranchisement found mostly racial stereotypes in the histories of their day.

Bias was normal. Even as Simon G. Atkins, a black educator, testified in 1901, "I do not believe that the white people of North Carolina have repudiated the spirit of Christ; . . . I do not believe that race hate can thrive in any considerable part of the state's soil," aversion, condescension, and contempt proceeded apace. Daniel Hill's *Young People's History of North Carolina*, a popular primer, virtually mocked Negro citizens with its caricature of the "Negro Mammy" and depiction of enslavement as a welfare system providing free housing and medical care. "As a rule the slaves were comfortably clothed, given an abundance of wholesome food, and kindly treated," though an occasional "bad-tempered" owner made their lot hard. "Cruel masters and cruel mistresses were scorned then just as men and women who treat animals cruelly are now scorned," it explained. "These slaves were brought into the colonies fresh from a savage life in Africa and in two or three generations were changed into respectable men and women. This fact shows, better than any words can, how prudently and how wisely they were managed." Other publications cast bondmen and freedmen in the role of menace. In a college-level syllabus, by historians William K. Boyd of Trinity College and J. G. de Roulhac Hamilton of the University of North Carolina, references to blacks were confined solely to topics treating the abolition era, Reconstruction, and Redemption, classic episodes in turmoil. In fact, R. D. W. Connor's *Ante-Bellum Builders of North Carolina*, an authoritative work, blamed Negro chattels for class conflict between "aristocratic planters" and "the 'common people.'"[5] The slave, rather than avarice or greed, was the problem.

Stereotypes survived, but little by little circumstances did enlighten historical inquiry. Dissenters, no matter how cautious, sometimes stirred a hornet's nest. Trinity College professor John Spencer Bassett is best remembered for calling Booker T. Washington the greatest Southerner next to Robert E. Lee, thereby infuriating racists and almost getting himself fired. Yet Bassett's earliest works, which are seldom mentioned, chronicled Tar Heel servitude and slavery, inching forward the long process of incorporating blacks into state history. By the time he went north to Smith College in 1906, a much-needed interracial dialogue had begun, thanks to his influence. Despite the color line, academic liberals and blacks like Simon G. Atkins did communicate. Another participant in that exchange was Charlotte Hawkins Brown, president of Palmer Memorial Institute, a school for black girls at Sedalia. Brown also led the statewide Federation of Colored Women's Clubs, whose motto, "Lifting as We Climb," echoed progressivism behind the color line. Her activities, and those of isolated Negro teachers in general, together with rural-to-urban migrations, especially during World War I, heightened public awareness of the black presence. Riots in Fayetteville and Winston-Salem attested to Negroes' escalating expectations, to 763,407 persons' postwar hopes.

Meanwhile, other developments improved knowledge about the Negro's past and present. The Institute for Research in Social Science, organized at the University of North Carolina in 1924 by sociologist Howard W. Odum, published several studies of Southern folk and racial traditions, including two volumes on Negro songs. Many of the songs had been collected in North Carolina. Helping to popularize black history and culture in the 1920s, too, was Negro History Week. The Association for the Study of Negro Life and History, founded at Chicago in 1915 and led by Dr. Carter G. Woodson, was national sponsor for the annual observance, an effort that hardly went unnoticed.[6] To wit, *The Story of Durham*, released by Duke University Press in 1927, devoted a whole chapter to the Negro.[7]

Gradually, during the 1930s, scholarly neglect of the Negro weakened. With crises in unemployment, relief, and civilian mobilization for national defense, the North Carolina Commission on Interracial Cooperation, which achieved statewide visibility in

Fig. 1-3. Charlotte Hawkins Brown, educator and founder of Palmer Memorial Institute, a boarding school at Sedalia, North Carolina. Photograph from files of the North Carolina Division of Archives and History, Raleigh.

1931 when it merged with the Virginia Commission, was kept very busy. Campaigns for reform, led by the commission as well as all-black groups, emerged against abuses in the farm-tenancy system, antiunion tactics in the textile and tobacco industries, racial discrimination in hiring, lynch law, and segregated schools. Each challenge, even when unsuccessful, increased public tolerance for change. In 1933, for example, state lawyers stalled the Durham NAACP's attempt to enroll a black student in the University of North Carolina. But the university's good reputation as a center of liberal scholarship contributed to more enlightened racial attitudes. Its *Journal of Social Forces* and outstanding press printed a number of sympathetic race relations studies. In this atmosphere of growing openness, less sympathetic but embarrassed writers began cloaking naked prejudice. "When first brought to this country they did not understand the ways or even the language of the white people," hedged a 1933 textbook by Alex Arnett. "But they were not entirely uncivilized. Before any of them had been taken from Africa they had developed a civilization of their own. . . . It was more like that of the Indians."[8]

Inevitably, through petition and protest, black higher education was upgraded. And Negro schools, whose professors and students could see beyond the blocked horizon, enhanced the recognition of Afro-American interests. These institutions employed and graduated a host of talented persons, including four who distinguished themselves as historians of the Afro-American experience. Helen G. Edmonds and John Hope Franklin were faculty members at North Carolina College. Benjamin Quarles and Earl E. Thorpe were alumni of Shaw and North Carolina College, respectively. As the events that followed Pearl Harbor increased the visibility of black Americans and the American dilemma disturbed peace at home, the university press at Chapel Hill brought out Franklin's study of Carolina free Negroes and an appraisal of contemporary Negro demands edited by black historian Rayford W. Logan.[9]

After World War II greater progress occurred in recognizing Negro heritage. The breakdown of the old order in the South and the creation of a new one made this a period, as H. G. Jones termed it, "where historians fear to tread."[10] Desegregation, nationally and regionally, revived the study of Negro history in the quest for African and Afro-American studies. Faced with the evidence of the black contribution to the state's history, even proud North Carolinians grappled with a multiracial view of their past.

The difficulty lay in the elaborate mythology of the state, a claim to moderation and progressivism that masked the depth of existing inequality. North Carolina emerged from "fighting for the four freedoms" incredibly optimistic, if shaky. The state had seen black-white confrontations, some of them fatal, but nothing like the bloodlettings at Alexandria, Louisiana, Columbia, Tennessee, or Detroit. Allegedly, compared to those of neighboring South Carolina and Virginia, Tar Heel Negroes enjoyed more advancement within the dual framework. They boasted ten four-year colleges, five state run and two offering graduate or professional degrees in agronomy, law, liberal arts, library science, and nursing. Fabled Durham, "Capital of the Black Middle Class," held its own, and a handful of colored communities in the Piedmont possessed a swing vote in their areas. Of course, hardcore racism remained. *From Slavery to Freedom*, written by John Hope Franklin and containing a plethora of Caroliniana, suggested why: "Too frequently the Negro's survival in America has depended on his capacity to adjust—indeed, to accommodate—himself to the dominant culture and the obstacles have at times been too great to permit him to make significant achievements in the usual sense of the word." The message went unheard. "Many see in North Carolina a closer approximation to national norms," hailed Harvard political scientist V. O. Key. "It enjoys a reputation for progressive outlook in many phases of life, especially industrial development, education, and race relations."[11] The myth was canonized. Consequently, the 1954 decision against school segregation in *Brown* v. *Board of Education* delivered a powerful shock.

Alienation and defiance grew, yet the Second Reconstruction encouraged criticism of the past. Big, thick *North Carolina: The History of a Southern State*, by Hugh Talmage Lefler and Albert Ray Newsome, stopped with 1953, finding no precedent for integration. "The idea of social equality was repugnant to most whites and was advocated by very few Negroes," concluded its post–Civil War section. "There was some talk about mixed schools, but this proposition did not meet with much approval." As if getting the hint, few of the Negro's friends celebrated desegregation. "In substance," sociologist Howard W. Odum stated, "here is a sudden demand for the white man, long conditioned in the Negro complex and Southern loyalties, bottomed in the long heritage of race prejudice and cultural evolution, to change . . . overnight." Coincidentally, just as America's past masters looked anew at slavery, Negroes were boycotting buses.[12]

Local reactions varied. Reflecting conservative pride, *Our North Carolina Heritage*, a photographic collection published by the National Society of the Children of the American Revolution of North Carolina, limited the Negro photographs to a black coachman, Johnson C. Smith University, a slave auction, the colored quarters, and little black Sambo eating watermelon. Pauli Murray's *Proud Shoes: The Story of an American Family*, on the other hand, traced four generations of her Fitzgerald relatives, old-line Durham blacks. After Chapel Hill rejected her for graduate work in 1939, the author won bachelor and master of laws degrees from Howard University and the University of California at Berkeley. "As a civil rights activist fighting against racial segregation when challengers of segregation policy were few and defeats were customary, I found it imperative to declare my American heritage," she insisted later. "Not Communism, but the ideals and influences within my own family had made me a lifelong fighter against all forms of inequality and injustice." Anticipating *Roots* by two decades, *Proud Shoes* employed biography and genealogy to recover "the story of a people involved in a crucial turning point in our nation's history."[13]

Still, it would take "creative disorder" to rip off the mask of moderation. When policemen and protesters clashed during the 1960s, turning the Piedmont into a battleground, North Carolina became leader and villain. Negro collegians, sharing the values while shifting the vision of their parents, defied Jim Crow. In February of 1960, North Carolina A&T's students launched sit-ins. By mid-April, those from Elizabeth City State Teachers College, St. Augustine's College, and Shaw University were helping to organize the Student Nonviolent Coordinating Committee. SNCC, as it was known, then planned statewide demonstrations by students from Barber-Scotia, Bennett, Livingstone, North Carolina College, Johnson C. Smith, Winston-Salem Teachers, and elsewhere. At least in the national press, Citizens' Councils, deployment of national guardsmen, and school bombings made matters look worse deeper south. But the abuse in 1963 and 1964 of black and white demonstrators in Greensboro and Chapel Hill, where 2,900 went to jail, anticipated the brutality of the 1965 march from Selma to Montgomery. Militants from Duke University and the Unversity of North Carolina at Chapel Hill sparked hospital and food-service workers' strikes in 1968 and 1969 that exposed both antiunionism and racism. And the Charlotte-Mecklenburg busing controversy, which the Supreme Court did not resolve until 1971 with a decision in favor of busing to achieve school desegregation, proved that quiet noncompliance could be more effective than massive resistance. Already journalists and novelists were peeling the state's moderate label. *The Free Men* portrayed an interracial coalition of Chapel Hill dissidents, perhaps a sign of things to come. *Lunch at the Five and Ten* put the A&T four in the spotlight, asking ironically, "What's going on down there? Nothing!"[14]

Much had happened in the sixties, and it spilled over into the seventies. In the wake of the assassination of Martin Luther King, Jr., and the Vietnam protests, the campuses became battlegrounds for change. Although ignored by administrators, Afro-American associations in the predominantly white institutions invoked slogans of "Black Power" and "Black Studies," the last to be implemented by developing black-oriented courses and recruiting black instructors.[15] As campus groups helped sharpen issues of culture and curriculum, outsiders reevaluated Carolina's racial record. The facade of liberalism, several found, obscured hate groups, intransigent racism, and political chicanery. The state "lagged behind various other border states in adopting measures of compliance, and a congressional investigation in the 1960s revealed that North Carolina now had more dues-paying members of the Ku Klux Klan than any other state," confirmed University of Kentucky historian Charles P. Roland. Two critics, Jack Bass and

Walter DeVries, characterized North Carolina as "perhaps the least changed of the old Confederate states." Michael Myerson, a Northerner and member of the Communist party, found the Old North State unbelievably repressive and violent: "Whatever one's guess of Klan influence, the cross burns bright in many a white Carolinian's heart."[16]

Some North Carolinians, less sanguine than ever, tried to deal with the paradox. Yes, they agreed, black Carolinians deserved their due. For a moment it seemed that somebody had heard attorney Johnson's plea. In addition to its usual slave and ex-slave installments, the revised edition of Hugh Lefler's *North Carolina History Told by Contemporaries* illustrated Negro education and progress during the interwar era as well as the course of race relations through Governor Terry Sanford's "Good Neighbor Council." A 1970 literary survey by Richard Walser included Negro writers Charles W. Chesnutt, James E. McGirt, and exciting Julia Fields. Ex-company president William Kennedy lauded North Carolina Mutual as the nation's top black business.[17] Even so, concern and insight varied. Whereas the 1973 version of Lefler and Newsome's *North Carolina* covered desegregation in two paragraphs, Walter Weare's social history of the North Carolina Mutual Life Insurance Company, published the same year, argued that "integration appeared as an inevitable good, and hence racial solidarity as a device whose days were numbered."[18] In the next few years studies were published on Indians and Negroes and the experience of blacks in revolutionary North Carolina, the latter a product of the bicentennial.[19] But it was the North Carolina Museum of History's year-long exhibition of artifacts, dioramas, displays, documents, and photographs, "arranged chronologically to tell the story of the state's black heritage," that most stimulated public interest.[20] Complementing the exhibit were the publication of the new textbook for the state's North Carolina history courses, *Carolina Quest*, which was more multiethnic in content than any previous text;[21] the founding of a black genealogy project at A&T; the instituting of new programs in the North Carolina Division of Archives and History;[22] and the recording of oral accounts of the activities of black communities.[23]

The task ahead is to improve on these efforts, to integrate North

Carolina history. During the 1980s studies on themes associated with the Civil Rights and Black Power movements should inform anew our inquiry into Tar Heel race relations. Beginning with colonial origins and moving to the present, broad-minded investigators will write about black culture as well as white attitudes. By describing how one-third of the people fared as unfree toilers and second-class citizens, they can reeducate the public about the state's past and revitalize scholarly endeavor to look at society from the bottom up. For as contributors and victims, blacks are the key to understanding colonialism and the American Revolution; enslavement and the Civil War; freedom and Jim Crow; the fight since *Brown*, and North Carolina "progressivism." As a step toward an integrated approach, and a preliminary step only, what follows is a general inventory of the record of black Carolinians.

Survey of the Literature of Black History in North Carolina

Although the era of exploration and settlement through 1700 is remote, it was formative. "Long before the region of Carolina was named for an English king, and generations before any English subject set foot there," Peter H. Wood writes, "people from West Africa were walking its sandy shoreline." Next to native Americans, Afro-Americans may be the oldest state residents. The image of those pioneer blacks, however, is vague. Colonial ethnohistorians who, according to College of William and Mary professor James Axtel, analyze the contact and shifting frontiers "between competing and sometimes cooperating ethnic groups— French, Dutch, English, Spanish, German, Swedish, African, and Indian," will discover an unplowed field here.[24]

The long presence of Africans in the area remains a fugitive subject. Reportedly, Spaniards brought them. Negroes accompanied and disrupted the 1526 coastal expedition of Lucas Vásquez de Ayllón, a known slave trader. By 1540 blacks had traveled further inland with Hernando de Soto. Angel de Villafañe's 1561 mission to Cape Hatteras enlisted them, while others built garrisons for Hernando Boyano and Juan Pardo, who explored the mountains. Periodically, the black servants escaped and took refuge within Indian tribes. Anglo-Spanish rivalry helped, too. It is possible that as many as three hundred Indians and two hundred Negroes, all captives from Francis Drake's raid in the Caribbean and Florida, absconded when his fleet rescued distressed English colonists from Roanoke Island in 1586.[25] Except for a few researchers, these matters are trivia. But they are important facts in early North Carolina ethnohistory.

The "Province of Carolana," like its neighbor to the north, obtained labor largely through human bondage. In the 1650s, when Virginia farmers, renegades, and traders trickled into the Albemarle Sound area, black bondmen and women came with them. Encouraging slavery, the Lords Proprietors granted headrights of fifty acres per chattel over age fourteen. The owner, they said, could exercise "absolute Authority over his Negro Slaves, of what opinion or Religion soever." If forced and free labor coexisted, the former soon dominated in importance. At the outset Virginians eyed Indians as a cheap work force, Edmund S. Morgan says, then switched to unpaid Africans. Carolinians had no plans to pay either group, and they preferred blacks. One proprietor echoed a common approach among masters when he declared, "In ye meane time I hope you will inquire after ye stocke wee have paid for, & place on ye Island if you see reason for it, & more whereby wee may have a quantity of Hoggs flesh, wch will soonest come to bare to send to Barbados wch will pduce us Neagroes & Sarvts: to rayse a plantacon."[26]

Two master's theses treat Africans in this developing domain. "The practice of slavery was limited in Albemarle," concludes Lindley Smith Butler, "and Indian slavery (which would cause future Indian wars) was as common as Negro slavery."[27] Susan H. Brinn suggests, on the other hand, that "from the beginning, the blacks' existence and freedom were circumscribed by social custom," yet they "benefitted from the colony's . . . unstable character by claiming a measure of autonomy and self-reliance." Assertive behavior, manumission, and freedom of movement about town were common, she notes. Occasionally, interracial marriages occurred, and black families seemed strong. Enslaved persons were only moderately stigmatized. Unhappily, in the aftermath of the Tuscarora wars a set of codes was promulgated that severely proscribed slaves. After 1715 racism deepened. "Fewer Indians still resided in the region for whites to capture and wars had opened trade with South Carolina where imported Africans were available in growing numbers."[28] Thus, quite early in the game, economic, military, and racial pressures pushed the Negro into a mudsill status.

The sources are intact for a larger synthesis. Basic and useful are nuggets on slave trading, Albemarle and Cape Fear runaways and maroons, and the retention by Negroes of Old World crafts, dances, dialects, festivals, instruments, and songs.[29] (Wood meshes such materials in his prize-winning book on black South Carolinians.)[30] Also, as the scholarship shows, Africans, Indians, and Europeans were in constant interaction, and each group contributed to the new cultural mix.[31] A search of seventeenth-century documents informed by the thesis of cultural exchange could uncover data to deepen our understanding of African retentions, black resistance, and white racism in North Carolina.[32] Too, with the abundance of county records in Raleigh,[33] a study along the lines of T. H. Breen and Stephen Innes's, "*Myne Owne Ground*," which discusses the fate of free blacks in Northampton County, Virginia, would be in order.[34]

The interaction of various cultures did little to elevate contemporary opinions of North Carolina. An Englishman in 1701 found "no settled Government among them." Theirs, he complained, "only tis a place which receives Pirates, Runaways, and Illegal Traders." A Virginia governor added, "Carolina (I meane the North part of it) always was and is the sinke of America, the Refuge of our Renegadoes."[35] The backward image endured, eventually shaping the conventional view of North Carolinians.[36] Still, they were willing parties in the caste and class practices of the day.

The evolution of a benighted colony into an independent state had its dark underside. Everybody felt the frontier's sting. Colonists battled each other, environmental hazards, and hostile natives who had occupied the land for generations. The fortunate survived, but ethnic and racial prejudice lingered, and with it color conflict. If the landless and poor planters suffered most, Negroes, the mules of the laboring class, wore a permanent harness, one which few escaped in the eighteenth century.

Unlike most of his generation, John Spencer Bassett openly deplored oppression, but he backed into the pitfall of prejudice. "Hard as the process was on the spirit of liberty in the black man," he pondered, "yet it is difficult to see how the aimless, good-natured, and improvident African could ever have been brought to plow, to sow, to reap, to study, and at length to create thought except for the tutelage of his slaveholding master."[37] The bias is unacceptable today, though to a surprising extent studies touching upon colonial slaves duplicate Bassett's concern with their geographic distribution and legal status.[38]

While current demographic research promises far more on Afro-Americans before the American Revolution, there is agreement that slavery steadily expanded.[39] Growth is a perennial theme.[40] Carolina's farms and fields required fewer slaves than did the South Carolina rice fields and Virginia plantations, and lacking good harbors or navigable rivers, the state looked to its neighbors for black imports. With chattels concentrated in an area from Albemarle along the Virginia border into the Lower Cape Fear River valley, however, North Carolina became an integral part of Atlantic seaboard slave society.[41] In 1705, historians Marvin L. Michael Kay and Lorin Lee Cary report, there were about 1,000 Negroes. Their number rose to roughly 6,000 in 1730, when they constituted one-fifth of the people. During the next quarter century the black population tripled, reaching 18,532 in 1755. Afterward, in a little over a decade, it increased dramatically—more than doubling to 40,641 by 1767. Blacks then made up 25 percent of all residents. In 1772 approximately 54 percent of the Negro populace was male. The 1790 census tabulated 5,041 free Negroes, 100,572 slaves, and 288,204 whites for the state; 31 percent of white families owned slaves.[42] By the end of the century three of every ten Tar Heels were blacks.

Slave trafficking and Indian-Negro contacts have received less attention overall than modes of forced labor. It is known that markets in South Carolina and Virginia supplied blacks to eastern

North Carolina via the coastal waters and overland marches.[43] But just how many is conjectural. For example, Kay and Cary contend that over 50 percent of slave population growth between 1755 and 1767 resulted from the slave trade, with 55 to 70 percent coming overland. Their findings seriously question whether the rapid rise in the number of slaves for those years may be explained, as certain scholars suggest, by natural increase. Also, if they are correct, another assumption—that prior to the Revolution the trade was inconsequential and relatively few blacks fresh from Africa or the West Indies entered the colony—must be revised.[44]

The topic of black-red relations, which Kenneth W. Porter addressed back in 1948[45] and which has been the focus of recent monographs elsewhere,[46] is begging investigation. Whether as allies in bondage, foes of runaways, frontier hunters, or nonwhite masters, the Catawba, Cherokee, Chowanoc, Hatteras, and Tuscarora encountered Negroes. Edenton physician John Brickell saw only strife between these outsiders. "They [the rebel slaves] generally fly to the Woods, but as soon as the Indians have Notice from the Christians of their being there they disperse them; killing some, others flying for Mercy to the Christians (whom they have injured) rather than fall into the others Hands, who have a natural aversion to the Blacks, and put them to death with the most exquisite Tortures they can invent, whenever they catch them."[47] Some natives bought European notions of conquest. The Cherokee, contends Clemson University historian Theda Perdue, "in their flight from 'savagery' adopted a system of plantation slavery." Its operations, however, have been best studied in Georgia.[48] And too little is known about cooperation between African immigrants and Indian tribesmen, especially their mutual cultural reinforcement.[49] In contrast, work patterns for the majority of slaves are better detailed: tobacco planting throughout the Piedmont, naval stores and rice cultivation in the Lower Cape Fear, and wheat growing further west. At the same time, black craftsmen performed almost every conceivable skilled task.[50]

To make the slaves toil from dawn to dusk—or otherwise conform—were the lash and the law; these instruments of control are examined in a number of studies. Codes regulated Negro labor, movement, and punishment.[51] Almost always, dominant interests

$50 Reward.

RANAWAY from the Subscriber, living in the county of Edgecombe, N. C. about eight miles north of Tarborough, on the 24th of August last, a negro fellow named WASHINGTON, about 24 years of age, 5 feet 8 or 10 inches high, dark complexion, stout built, and an excellent field hand—no particular marks about him recollected. The said fellow was formerly owned by Mr. Jas. Taylor, of Martin county, and I think it more than probable that he is now lurking in the neighborhood of Taylor's Ferry. The above reward of *Fifty Dollars,* will be given to any person who will apprehend said negro and deliver him to me, or lodge him in jail so that I get him again. All persons are hereby forbid harboring or employing said fellow under penalty of the law.

JOHN LAWRENCE.

Oct. 4, 1827.

Fig. 1-4. Advertisements for runaway slaves appeared frequently in southern newspapers. This one was published in the 6 October 1827 issue of the *Free Press* (Tarborough). From the files of the North Carolina Division of Archives and History, Raleigh.

undercut blacks' security within the statutes. For example, compensations for executed slaves, 25 percent of public claims from 1748 to 1772, offset planters' losses in capital cases. As a cost-saving device, male first offenders, unless accused of murder or rape, were castrated in lieu of execution.[52] In general, black judge A. Leon Higginbotham, Jr., believes, "the law itself had created the mores of racial repression."[53] A callous disregard of black life persisted. When an uncommonly brave Tar Heel jurist denounced the doctrine "that it is not murder for a white man to kill a Negro slave," nobody heeded him. Yet despite the punishment system, "slave crimes" increased. The intense individualism of the average Carolina master, plus slaves' acts of accommodation and assertiveness, undermined law enforcement and slave surveillance. While literate bondmen and freemen sued in the courts, Negroes in towns used "rioting" and "caballing" to block curfews.[54] Fortunately, in their forthcoming book Kay and Cary will analyze the nature of Negro nonconformity.[55] Slave criminality may have been a recurrent form of resistance.

Writings treating the tribulations of slaveholding vary and, like most of the literature heretofore cited, yield only black reflections. But they gauge the ideological impact of the peculiar institution and measure its insidious power. Supposedly, old-line enclaves of settlers broke with a humanistic past, compromised principle, and pursued the material benefits of slavery. Burke County's English, Germans, and Scotch-Irish were acquisitive, never torn by moral questions. By contrast, the Germans of Forsyth and Rowan counties proved conscience-ridden. Slowly, we learn from Philip Africa, the Moravians moved from "gemeinschaft to gesellschaft," that is, self-sufficiency to capitalism, and "adapted their beliefs and community life to the prevailing mores of the region."[56] The neighboring Quakers seemed truly reluctant. According to Peter Kent Opper, friends disagreed internally, fought unsuccessful manumission battles against the legislature, and ultimately placed 350 blacks in a "trustee slaveholding system," at least until a deportation plan could be determined.[57] Whether blacks were willing converts in the course of the experiment or doubted what Wood terms "the political and religious merits of Christianity" has not been discussed.[58] Other than in a few devout souls, though, antislavery sentiment rarely surfaced. To most whites the marriage between bondage and freedom appeared compatible. White residents of Edgecombe County did a brisk business in dark flesh; over half the families boasted blacks. "Quite frequently slaves were slain both accidentally and premeditatedly," James K. Turner, author of a 1916 Trinity College Historical Society Paper, states. Servile "negro uprisings were especially dreaded." Violent control was emblematic of a powerful proslavery creed. It outlasted the Regulation and the Revolution.[59]

For the dialectic between black initiative and white power, contemporary observers are invaluable. A context of fear, hatred, and uncertainty is conveyed in the remarks of white witnesses, whether residents or travelers. Brickell said Africans possessed "barbarous and stubborn Natures." Scottish visitor Janet Schaw reported, "They steal whatever they can come at and even intercept the cows and milk them. They are indeed the constant plague of their tyrants."[60] Negro testimony, which evoked self-direction and struggle, may be harder to cull for this period. Job Ben Solomon and Olaudah Equiano published narratives detailing how they were kidnapped in West Africa and sold into Maryland and Virginia slavery.[61] While such accounts are unavailable for eighteenth-century black Carolinians, illustrations of their views on faith and freedom have been collected.[62] For example, in the earliest black petition to Congress, four North Carolina runaways decried the Fugitive Slave Act, asking, "Is not some remedy for an evil of such magnitude highly worthy of the deep inquiry and unfeigned zeal of the supreme Legislative Body of a free and enlightened people?"[63] Racial thought is crucial in the era of the American Revolution because, as Ira Berlin states, "by the 1770s, if not earlier, the vast majority of blacks were native Americans with no firsthand knowledge of Africa."[64]

Of great value on North Carolina is Jeffrey J. Crow's *Black Experience in Revolutionary North Carolina*. His book introduces a host of black characters and their strides toward freedom. (An appendix lists hitherto nameless Continental Negro soldiers). Armed with the assumption "that Afro-Americans were active, not passive, beings who in the face of unremitting adversity struggled to maintain their dignity," Crow discusses—against a back-drop of African culture, Christian conversion, and revolutionary philosophy—varieties of black insurgency: arson, assault, malingering, murder, poisoning, running away, and sabotage.[65] In an excellent sequel he shows that during and after the War for Independence patterns of rebelliousness shifted. The temporary weakening of caste structures heightened bondmen's hopes and multiplied instances of collective revolt, culminating in the widespread insurrection plots of 1800–1802.[66] These works, combined with discussions of the efforts of free blacks to handle legal proscription and those of slaves to develop familial, kinship, and sexual norms, belie charges of Negro passivity.[67]

Sectionalism and slavery, the Civil War, Reconstruction, a nation reunited under a banner of freedom and equality—all these are key parts in the Afro-American story. But in the traditional retellings the Negro is the proverbial "man in the middle," less an actor than an issue, whose importance depends upon the interests of northern and southern whites. Although revisionist historians in recent years have recast segments of it, much of this mythic script is intact. The real Afro-American experience in these years is still waiting to be recovered and written.

Standard overviews give only glimpses of antebellum black Carolinians as people. Bassett's is essentially a legal tract. "One law after another was passed which bore hardly on the slave, until at last he was bound hand, foot, and brain in the power of his master," the professor states, adding, "The chief cause . . . was the invention of the cotton gin and the consequent opening up of the cotton industry." Guion Griffis Johnson is dated in assuming that "for the most part, the planter found his slaves 'submissive' and 'robust for work.'" Nevertheless, her book is a careful consideration of slave labor and life, describing, with uncanny insight, diet and health, family relations, education and recreation, religion and resistance.[68] Overlooking these social categories, modern monographs on the state's plantation system have paid more attention to economic indices.[69] Yet earlier, James H. Boykin and James H. Brewer, of St. Augustine's and North Carolina College, respectively, had offered factual reminders that not just

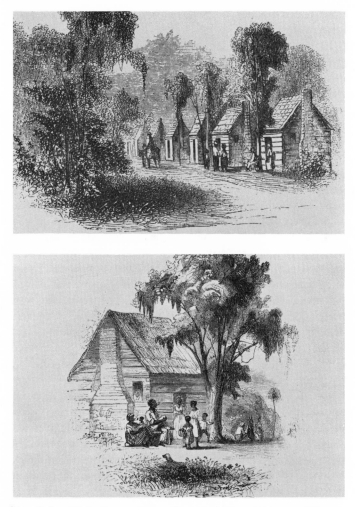

Figs. 1-5 and 1-6. Slave quarters. From T. Addison Richards, "The Rice Lands of the South," *Harper's New Monthly Magazine* 19 (November 1859): 724, 730.

black brawn but human beings underlay the Tar Heel cotton and tobacco kingdom.[70]

Its planter-rulers did more than collect profits; they limited freedom of thought. "Slavery absolute—nothing short of it—and as few free negroes as possible; that was the idea," according to Bassett.[71] Contributors to the study of antebellum slavery outline the situation accordingly. Proslavery spokesmen were right at home, while their opponents, especially after insurrection scares in 1830–1831, were driven out or silenced.[72] The court emerged in defense of white supremacy, but there was social strain.[73] Angry nonslaveholders contested planters' privileges, although both groups shared in their Negrophobia.[74] Colonizationists, whose ranks included slave owners, were tolerated—as were moralists who stayed within certain bounds.[75] Abolitionists, part of what Carl N. Degler calls the "Other South," remained an ostracized minority. In response, many Quakers left the state.[76] Of the studies on slavery in particular counties, the best is on Burke. Examining small-farm slavery in the upland tier, Edward Phifer finds that not all masters were rapists or sadists. The slaves, too, were accommodating, opportunistic, and rebellious. Onslow's blacks demonstrated a similar complexity. To maximize security every locale maintained a slave patrol.[77]

In order to see inside the black world, one must collate a patchwork of perspectives. Whether slaves were Sambos, as some historians claim and others deny, is no longer a burning issue. Fortunately, though, the argument blessed us with a revisionist revival that inspired recognition of slave communities and sources.[78] Despite the matchless holdings of Research Triangle libraries, however, nobody working in this new genre has done a history of the bondmen in North Carolina.[79] Rather, they crop up in general collections and interpretations as abolitionists, artisans, autobiographers, chambermaids, coachmen, fugitives, narrators, rebels, and preachers.[80] If it were possible to combine these references and incorporate them with what archaeologists are finding on material culture at state historic sites like Somerset and Stagville plantations, the results could be rewarding.[81] For the moment, the facts are dispersed.

A matter needing clarification is Negroes' activism. They constituted a third of the population, with never more than 3 percent of them free. Though Virginia and South Carolina had larger numbers, North Carolina adopted the most elaborate, and perhaps stringent, Negro code. Was it because bondmen were ungovernable that authorities tried constant control—the law and patrol—to preserve order? In a 1928 article, Rosser H. Taylor contends that white fear outweighed tangible evidence of black conspiracy.[82] But Herbert Aptheker's later analysis of slave revolts contradicts that view. Aspiration and desperation drove slaves to rebel, and Aptheker found eleven encounters of statewide significance between 1803 and 1830. When in 1829 David Walker, a Wilmington-born free Negro expatriate, published *Walker's Appeal*, which called upon slaves to revolt, black unrest increased. During the three decades afterward, atrocities in Bladen, Burke, Craven, Hyde, Nash, Onslow, and Pitt counties could be traced to black resistance and white retaliation.[83] A 1946 master's thesis (supervised by John Hope Franklin) complements Aptheker's conclusions, illustrating that runaways disrupted and frightened white society.[84] A sense of continuity in slave insurgency, nonetheless, is absent—and this should be a fruitful topic for research.[85]

Similarly, since Franklin's seminal study a generation ago, little has been written on the changing fortunes of free blacks. So the beleaguered generation of John Chavis, educator, Thomas Day, cabinetmaker, Lunsford Lane, vendor, and Catherine Stanly, seamstress, warrants further inquiry, particularly in a study of freemen's role in organized protest.[86] According to W. E. B. Du Bois, in 1861, prior to secession, two thousand bondmen and freemen fled the state.[87] When the guns were fired at Sumter, therefore, racial battle lines had already been drawn.

That the war marked a momentous turning point is of course cliché. Afro-Americans in blue and gray, Federal and Confederate policies, emancipation and its effects—all are subjects of vital interest. The literature focusing on blacks, however, is modest.[88] As the fighting wore on, class and race pressures mounted within the state, sharpening poor white disaffection with the war effort and black slave disloyalty. Predictably, proud Carolina voted against a measure to arm and free the slaves, a last-ditch effort to preserve independence by sacrificing slavery.[89] James H.

Brewer's *The Confederate Negro*, documenting Virginia's extensive use of colored military laborers, embraces North Carolina.[90] Some black attitudes contain surprises here,[91] although fleeing bondmen helped to drive planters westward, intensify masters' demands for security, and topple the Tar Heel Confederacy.[92] A bittersweet encounter between blacks and bluecoats, Union deployment of contrabands as soldiers and workers, and the Negro's new vision have been described.[93] But the freedom experiment at Roanoke Island deserves better coverage; it was a dress rehearsal for Reconstruction.[94]

Citizenship and enfranchisement were moments of possibility, however short-lived. If traditional prejudice against black participation in politics is passé,[95] the ballot and officeholding still dominate historiography.[96] Or, others—northern missionaries, Republicans, southern churchmen—are praised for advancing a backward race.[97] But in his landmark book, W. E. B. Du Bois emphasized self-help, and that trait is evident in Robert G. Fitzgerald, a former Union soldier who founded a colored school at Hillsborough, fought the Ku Klux Klan, and eventually opened a brickyard in Durham.[98] Through him we get a personal portrayal of Negro life. Happily, some students of Reconstruction do notice this dimension, and current research is promising.[99]

From the 1870s through the turn of the century North Carolina increased its campaign to drive the Negro, in Du Bois's words, "back toward slavery." While political and race relations studies for this period far outnumber those on the internal life of the black community, several are scholarly and stress blacks as actors.[100] We are significantly indebted to Frenise A. Logan for his statewide synthesis and a number of articles on broader developments.[101] Some of these topics—business enterprise,[102] deprivation within the crop-lien system,[103] educational inequality,[104] migration,[105] racial segregation,[106] and religion[107]—are also pursued elsewhere. They are synthesized in Sydney Nathans's *The Quest for Progress*, an overview that combines first-person accounts with photographs of historic sites.[108]

To date the schoolhouse is less visible in writings concerning this period than the statehouse, and both block our view of eastern Carolina fields, where a mass Negro peasantry lived in the shadow of the plantation.[109] The church is celebrated, but its functions are ambiguous.[110] Biographical profiles are mostly of businessmen and politicians such as John Merrick and George H. White.[111] Educators like Simon G. Atkins, Charles N. Hunter, and Edward A. Johnson are neglected, but Hunter is profiled in a 1981 dissertation. Their female contemporaries—Charlotte Hawkins Brown, Anna Julia Cooper, Annie W. Holland—are also neglected, though Brown and Cooper are the subjects of recent theses.[112] Such teachers and thinkers, the first college-trained generation, exemplify the mind of the newly emancipated Negro world.

A survey of twentieth-century North Carolina black history reveals two major problems with the existing scholarship. First, it seems to leap from the 1890s to the 1960s. We have many titles on slavery, Reconstruction and after, the Populist-Progressive battles that caused the Wilmington riot and constitutional disfranchisement, and post-*Brown* civil rights, but historiography bypasses the age of segregation. Since black responses to Jim Crow set the stage for the Second Reconstruction and shaped the later racial revolt, this gap is critical. Second, studies of desegregation generally employ a top-down approach, with national leadership and legislation dwarfing local initiative and struggle. Often, the ordinary persons who took risks and made sacrifices are overlooked. Perhaps recent works and others in progress will help to correct these flaws.

Certain categories of Negro life need immediate attention. (A survey of the half-century before *Brown* would be welcome. For the time being, we must rely upon monographs which are no longer suitable.)[113] Business claims a well-written book: the thesis is that North Carolina Mutual's line on racial solidarity, backed by sensible management, insured its economic success.[114] Beyond insurance, however, the historiography of black enterprise is unpenetrated. Education, from the standpoint of state discrimination, is described ably.[115] The internal view of black education is less satisfactory. Frequently, such studies simply eulogize, and comments on the mission of their schools, including how race affected instruction and student life, are low key. College histories, by the same token, merely recite administrative facts.[116] Studies of folk, literary, and musical expressions can illumine the community behind the Jim Crow wall, but so far Negro culture eludes Tar Heel historians.[117] The topic of migration is unmined, although approximately 133,000 Negroes went north, and thousands more deserted fields for factories; blacks made up over a third of North Carolina urban dwellers by 1940, yet they are virtually invisible.[118] Fortunately, oral history projects have begun to record the stories of many black migrants to Piedmont cities.[119] Politics, meanwhile, boasts a handful of volumes whose net contents explain impediments to black voting.[120] Religion is handled fragmentarily, even though the church may have been the moving force in the Negro's spiritual and temporal survival.[121] Installments on race relations cover all aspects of institutional and intellectual life, the most typical relating white attitudes[122] and practices.[123] Some emphasize Negro strivings.[124] None traces Negro ideology and strategy, culminating in the attack on segregation during World War II. This was a regional phenomenon, and black Carolinians were among its principal architects. Also, key events in the pre-*Brown* revolt occurred in North Carolina.[125]

But for William Chafe's *Civilities and Civil Rights*, winner of the Mayflower Cup as the best book of North Carolina nonfiction, the postwar years to the sit-ins and the present would be a maze. Examining Greensboro in "a time span of three decades . . . to gain historical perspective on the relationship between blacks and whites and the development of different levels of protest," Chafe creates an important synthesis. Combining oral and written sources, though favoring the former, and minimizing "the history of civil rights organizations, the impact of federal legislation, and the significance of leaders like Martin Luther King, Jr.," he discusses "the day-to-day life of the local people most affected by the movement."[126] Attempts to apply or complement this methodology are few. Marcellus Barksdale, a graduate student in the Duke Oral History Program, where Chafe was codirector, compares black activism in Weldon, Chapel Hill, and Monroe from 1946 to 1965; Aingred Dunston portrays protest in Winston-Salem.[127] Several other authors stress the role of the middle-class Negro vanguard.[128] Dramatic incidents, including demonstrations, furnish titles for several descriptive and popular accounts.[129] Eye opening, if top down in point of view, are social science studies on school desegregation attitudes and policy.[130] The North Carolina experience with SNCC, Afro-American studies, and Black Power is unchronicled, but black labor, union organizing, and other working-class issues that involve the black commuity have become themes.[131]

My conclusions are guarded, as much depends upon what happens in the 1980s. This survey is based upon a potpourri of writings, a large number of them unpublished. It indicates that overall there has been progress in black North Carolina historiography. Without further development, however, the possibilities for a fuller synthesis of the North Carolina experience will dim. In whole periods of the state's nearly four-hundred-year odyssey the black contribution is unchronicled, and much in blacks' contacts with Indians and whites, their cultural evolution, their activism in bondage and freedom, their separate institutional and intellectual life under segregation, and their quest for desegregation and equality remains obscure. Indeed, many twists and turns in the Negro's path to the present have not been analyzed simply because they are unperceived.

The challenge is complex. Attorney Johnson laid the blame at the doorstep of white historians, whose works were altogether biased and capricious. In the intrepid schoolmaster's day, and a long time after him for that matter, the remedy was simple: acknowledgment of Negro contributions. But the post–World War II age not only saw a move toward better treatment of blacks in histories but also sharpened demands for a democratic interpretation of North Carolina's past. Hence, the lion's share of the extant scholarship on the black experience in the state has been produced since the 1960s, with the North Carolina Division of Archives and History and Museum of History providing conspicuous support. Officially, nonrecognition of blacks is passé. The problem now is on another level. It relates to the challenge of incorporating Afro-Americans into a holistic interpretation of American history. In North Carolina it is the task of integrating the experience of the black minority into the established history of the state.

Closing his splendid review of the literature in early black history that appeared from 1960 to 1976, Peter Wood drives home this point:

> We have scarcely begun to consider how these recent studies . . . could inspire, or alter, future work on obviously related subjects. It has been the historiographic achievement of the era since 1960 to draw forth a mass of detailed monographic material on early Afro-Americans that far exceeds all previous work combined. While these studies, some of which continue to appear, represent a considerable accomplishment in their own right, they pose an even larger challenge for the years ahead. The task now at hand—a difficult one intellectually and politically for all concerned— involves integrating newly detailed evidence on Afro-American beginnings into the broader story of colonialism in America.[132]

Black Carolina, carefully studied, should illumine our portrait of North Carolina. Of course, the finished product may look quite different from traditional views of the state. In the publications of professionals like Eric Anderson, James Brewer, William Chafe, Jeffrey Crow, Helen Edmonds, John Hope Franklin, Michael Kay and Lee Cary, Frenise Logan, and Howard Rabinowitz, we get some important broad strokes. The work of others, mainly graduate students, is helping to fill in and balance that picture, for example, by checking the predominance of accounts that merely chronicle white attitudes over those that attempt to discover and analyze the core of black culture. Conversion of theses and dissertations into articles and books is crucial to reshaping public knowledge. Scholars and students in this decade might well determine if we will have an integrated, multiracial state history. If their labors are encouraged and sustained, North Carolina yet may be redeemed from its "sin of omission."

NOTES

1. Edward A. Johnson, *A School History of the Negro Race in America, from 1619 to 1890* (Raleigh: Edwards & Broughton, 1890), pp. 3–4.

2. See E. A. Johnson's obituary in the *New York Times*, 25 July 1944, and his biographical sketch in *Who's Who in Colored America, 1941–44* (New York: Thomas Yenser, 1944), p. 285. For Wright, see Peter H. Wood, "'I Did the Best I Could for My Day': The Study of Early Black History during the Second Reconstruction, 1960 to 1976," *William and Mary Quarterly*, 3d ser., 35 (April 1978): 185–86, and R. R. Wright, "The Migration of Negroes to the North," *Annals* 27 (May 1906): 559–78. Cf. James Weldon Johnson, *Along This Way: The Autobiography of James Weldon Johnson* (1933; reprint ed., New York: Viking, 1968), pp. 62–66, 214. He wrote of Atlanta University, p. 66, "I perceived that education for me meant, fundamentally: preparation to meet the tasks and exigencies of life as a Negro, a realization of the peculiar responsibilities due to my own racial group, and a comprehension of the application of American democracy to Negro citizens. . . . Students talked 'race.' It was the subject of essays, orations, and debates. Nearly all that was acquired, mental and moral, was destined to be fitted into a particular system of which 'race' was the center." E. A. Johnson's statement on capitalizing the word *Negro* is in *A School History*, p. 5.

3. Cf. George Washington Williams, *History of the Negro Race in America from 1619 to 1880*, 2 vols. (New York: Putnam, 1883); and Johnson, *A School History*, esp. pp. 12–13, 38–40, 51, 87–94, 145, 150, 166–77, 192. Also, see the comments on Johnson's book in John Hope Franklin, "The Future of Negro History," *University of Chicago Magazine* 62 (January–February 1970): 15–21.

4. His literary and political achievements are discussed in the Johnson obituary, *New York Times*, above; Florette Henri, *Black Migration: Movement North, 1900–1920* (Garden City, N.Y.: Doubleday, 1975), p. 207; and Durham *Sun*, 23 March 1983. The quotations are from Edward A. Johnson, *History of Negro Soldiers in the Spanish-American War* (Raleigh: Capital Printing Company, 1899), p. 213; and E. A. Johnson, *Light Ahead for the Negro* (New York: Grafton Press, 1904), p. v.

5. S. G. Atkins, "The Situation in North Carolina," *Southern Workman* 30 (April 1901): 199; Daniel Harvey Hill, *Young People's History of North Carolina* (Charlotte: Stone and Barringer Company, 1907), pp. 102–3; William K. Boyd and J. G. de Roulhac Hamilton, *A Syllabus of*

North Carolina History, 1584–1876 (Durham: Seeman Printery, 1913); R. D. W. Connor, *Ante-Bellum Builders of North Carolina* (Raleigh: North Carolina State Normal & Industrial College, 1914), pp. 24–25.

6. See John Spencer Bassett, "Stirring up the Fires of Racial Antipathy," *South Atlantic Quarterly* 2 (October 1903): 297–305. Among Bassett's earliest works are *Slavery and Servitude in the Colony of North Carolina* (Baltimore: Johns Hopkins Press, 1896) and *Slavery in the State of North Carolina* (Baltimore: Johns Hopkins Press, 1899). A helpful sketch of Bassett is in William S. Powell, ed., *Dictionary of North Carolina Biography* (Chapel Hill: University of North Carolina Press, 1979), 1:107–8. Black educators and black-white relations are treated by Raymond Gavins, "Black Leadership in North Carolina to 1900," in Jeffrey J. Crow and Robert E. Winters, Jr., eds., *The Black Presence in North Carolina* (Raleigh: North Carolina Museum of History, 1978), pp. 1, 5, 7; and by Tera W. Hunter, "A Biographical Study of Charlotte Hawkins Brown: Unearthing One of the Many Brave," honors essay, Duke University, 1982. For the black population in 1920, check *Fourteenth Census of the United States: 1920 State Compendium North Carolina* (Washington, D.C.: Government Printing Office, 1925). On the Institute for Research in Social Science, consult Guy Benton Johnson and Guion Griffis Johnson, *Research in Service to Society: The First Fifty Years of the Institute of Research in Social Science at the University of North Carolina* (Chapel Hill: University of North Carolina Press, 1980), pp. ix, 131–37; and Katherine Jocher et al., eds., *Folk, Region, and Society: Selected Papers of Howard W. Odum* (Chapel Hill: University of North Carolina Press, 1964), pp. vii–viii. The volumes of Negro songs were Howard W. Odum and Guy B. Johnson, *The Negro and His Songs* (Chapel Hill: University of North Carolina Press, 1925), and Howard W. Odum and Guy B. Johnson, *Negro Workaday Songs* (Chapel Hill: University of North Carolina Press, 1926). On the Association for the Study of Negro Life and History and Carter G. Woodson, see David C. Roller and Robert W. Twyman, eds., *The Encyclopedia of Southern History* (Baton Rouge: Louisiana State University Press, 1979), p. 1358.

7. William Kenneth Boyd, *The Story of Durham: City of the New South* (Durham: Duke University Press, 1927), pp. 277–97.

8. The state interracial commission is considered in Augustus Merrimon Burns III, "North Carolina and the Negro Dilemma, 1930–1950," Ph.D. diss., University of North Carolina at Chapel Hill, 1969. Reform movements affecting North Carolina are detailed in George B. Tindall, *The Emergence of the New South, 1913–1945* (Baton Rouge:

Louisiana State University Press, 1967). The NAACP's lawsuit is discussed by Richard Kluger, *Simple Justice: The History of Brown v. Board of Education and Black America's Struggle for Equality* (New York: Vintage Books, 1977), pp. 155–58; and National Association for the Advancement of Colored People, *Twenty-fourth Annual Report* (New York: NAACP, 1934), pp. 18–19. For liberalism at the university, see Johnson and Johnson, *Research in Service to Society*, pp. 35–43, 135–44; and Jocher et al., eds., *Folk, Region, and Society*, pp. vii–xi. The quote is from Alex Mathews Arnett, *The Story of North Carolina* (Chapel Hill: University of North Carolina Press, 1933), p. 284.

9. An evaluation of North Carolina black higher education is in Charles S. Johnson, *The Negro College Graduate* (Chapel Hill: University of North Carolina Press, 1938), pp. 23, 96, 140, 260–61. Also, see John Hope Franklin, *The Free Negro in North Carolina, 1790–1860* (Chapel Hill: University of North Carolina Press, 1943), and Rayford W. Logan, ed., *What the Negro Wants* (Chapel Hill: University of North Carolina Press, 1944). The shock of Logan's work prompted W. T. Couch to demur in a publisher's introduction, p. xx: "I believe that if complete elimination of segregation could be accomplished overnight— as many of the authors of this volume assume it ought to be—the consequences would be disastrous for everyone and more so for the Negro than the white man."

10. See H. G. Jones's chapter in Jeffrey J. Crow and Larry E. Tise, eds., *Writing North Carolina History* (Chapel Hill: University of North Carolina Press, 1979), pp. 191–220.

11. Walter B. Weare, *Black Business in the New South: A Social History of the North Carolina Mutual Life Insurance Company* (Urbana: University of Illinois Press, 1973), pp. 58, 265–78; John Hope Franklin, *From Slavery to Freedom: A History of American Negroes* (New York: Knopf, 1947), pp. xi–xii; V. O. Key, *Southern Politics in State and Nation* (New York: Vintage, 1949), pp. 205–13.

12. Hugh Talmage Lefler and Albert Ray Newsome, *North Carolina: The History of a Southern State* (Chapel Hill: University of North Carolina Press, 1954), p. 451; Jocher et al., eds., *Folk, Region, and Society*, p. 82. The link between historical inquiry and human rights struggle is suggested by David Brion Davis, "Slavery and the Post–World War II Historians," in Sidney W. Mintz, ed., *Slavery, Colonialism, and Racism* (New York: Norton, 1974), pp. 1–16.

13. Charlotte Ivey Hastings, comp., *Our North Carolina Heritage* (n.p.: National Society of the Children of the American Revolution of North Carolina, 1956), pp. 57, 60–62, 72, 135, 200; and the introduc-

tion to Pauli Murray, *Proud Shoes: The Story of an American Family* (New York: Harper, 1956). Another family history is Norma Jean and Carole Darden, *Spoonbread and Strawberry Wine: Recipes and Reminiscences of a Family* (Garden City, N.Y.: Doubleday, Anchor, 1978).

14. For the sit-ins and other demonstrations, including the role of SNCC, see William H. Chafe, *Civilities and Civil Rights: Greensboro, North Carolina, and the Black Struggle for Equality* (New York: Oxford University Press, 1980), pp. 71–101; and especially Capus M. Waynick et al., eds., *North Carolina and the Negro* (Raleigh: Mayors' Co-operating Committee, 1964), a report, replete with pictures, on black protest against legal segregation in fifty-five municipalities. The Duke and UNC at Chapel Hill workers' strikes are covered in Leah J. Wise, "Stirring the Pot: Oliver Harvey's Narrative Account of the Struggle to Organize Duke University," M.A. paper, Duke University, 1980. *Desegregation: How Schools Are Meeting Historic Challenge* (Arlington, Va.: National School Public Relations Association, n.d.), p. 77, considers the Charlotte-Mecklenburg case. Also, see John Ehle, *The Free Men* (New York: Harper, 1965), p. ix; and Miles Wolff, *Lunch at the Five and Ten: The Greensboro Sit-Ins* (New York: Stein and Day, 1970), p. 11.

15. Robert H. Brisbane, *Black Activism: Racial Revolution in the United States, 1954–1970* (Valley Forge, Pa.: Judson Press, 1974), pp. 223–44, gives an overview of post-1968 campus unrest and issues. For black studies in two black and five white North Carolina universities, read the *Asheville Citizen-Times*, 16 March 1969; Raleigh *News and Observer*, 27 April 1969; and Durham *Morning Herald*, 9 June 1969.

16. Charles P. Roland, *The Improbable Era: The South since World War II* (Lexington: University Press of Kentucky, 1975), pp. 30–42; Jack Bass and Walter DeVries, *The Transformation of Southern Politics: Social Change and Political Consequence since 1945* (New York: Basic Books, 1976), pp. 218–47; Michael Myerson, *Nothing Could Be Finer* (New York: International Publishers, 1978), p. 6. Unflattering, too, are William Bagwell, *School Desegregation in the Carolinas: Two Case Studies* (Columbia: University of South Carolina Press, 1972), pp. 119–25; Earl Black, *Southern Governors and Civil Rights: Racial Segregation as a Campaign Issue in the Second Reconstruction* (Cambridge: Harvard University Press, 1976), pp. 106–13, 294–96; and Neil R. McMillen, *The Citizens' Council: Organized Resistance to the Second Reconstruction, 1954–1964* (Urbana: University of Illinois Press, 1971), pp. 111–21, 310.

17. Hugh T. Lefler, ed., *North Carolina History Told by Contemporaries*, 4th ed. rev. enl. (Chapel Hill: University of North Carolina Press, 1965); Richard Walser, *Literary North Carolina: A Brief Historical Survey* (Raleigh: Department of Archives and History, 1970); William J. Kennedy, Jr., *The North Carolina Mutual Story: A Symbol of Progress, 1898–1970* (Durham: North Carolina Mutual Life Insurance Company, 1970).

18. Lefler and Newsome, *North Carolina*, 3d ed., pp. 695–96; Weare, *Black Business*, pp. 280–87.

19. *Paths toward Freedom: A Biographical History of Blacks and Indians in North Carolina* (Raleigh: Center for Urban Affairs at North Carolina State University, 1976); Jeffrey J. Crow, *The Black Experience in Revolutionary North Carolina* (Raleigh: Department of Cultural Resources, 1977).

20. "The Black Presence in North Carolina," 30 September 1978–31 August 1979, featured a book of essays, cited in n. 6; an interpretive brochure; a mobile museum rendition of the exhibit; and a phonograph album entitled *Eight-Hand Sets & Holy Steps*.

21. Thomas C. Parramore, *Carolina Quest* (Englewood Cliffs, N.J.: Prentice-Hall, 1978).

22. The appointment of the division's Afro-American history coordinator was announced in *Carolina Comments* 28 (November 1980): 147. See also Thornton W. Mitchell, *Preliminary Guide to Records Relating to Blacks in the North Carolina State Archives*, Archives Information Circular No. 17 (Raleigh: Department of Cultural Resources, 1980); and Earl E. Thorpe, *The Uses of Black History* (Raleigh: Department of Cultural Resources, 1980).

23. Examples are Chafe, *Civilities and Civil Rights*; and Marcellus Chandler Barksdale, "The Indigenous Civil Rights Movement and Cultural Change in North Carolina: Weldon, Chapel Hill, and Monroe, 1946–1965," Ph.D. diss., Duke University, 1977.

24. Peter H. Wood, *Black Majority: Negroes in Colonial South Carolina from 1670 through the Stono Rebellion* (New York: Norton, 1974), p. 3; James Axtell, "The Ethnohistory of Early America: A Review Essay," *William and Mary Quarterly*, 3d ser., 35 (January 1978): 110.

25. These facts are in Lefler and Newsome, *North Carolina*, pp. 4–5, 8; Wood, *Black Majority*, pp. 3–6; Edmund S. Morgan, *American Slavery—American Freedom: The Ordeal of Colonial Virginia* (New York: Norton, 1975), pp. 34–35, 41–42; and William S. Powell, *The North Carolina Colony* (New York: Macmillan, 1969), p. 10.

26. See Lefler and Newsome, *North Carolina*, p. 13; Mattie Erma

Edwards Parker et al., eds., *The Colonial Records of North Carolina, Second Series* (Raleigh: State Department of Archives and History, 1963), 1:150; Morgan, *American Slavery—American Freedom*, pp. 22–24, 239; and William S. Powell, ed., *Ye Countie of Albemarle in Carolina: A Collection of Documents, 1664–1675* (Raleigh: State Department of Archives and History, 1958), p. 7.

27. Lindley Smith Butler, "Life in Albemarle County, Carolina, 1663–1689," M.A. thesis, University of North Carolina at Chapel Hill, 1964, p. 45.

28. Susan H. Brinn, "Blacks in Colonial North Carolina, 1660–1689," M.A. thesis, University of North Carolina at Chapel Hill, 1978, pp. ix–x, 16, 23–57, 94–96, 105–13.

29. On slave trading, see John W. Blassingame, *The Slave Community: Plantation Life in the Ante-Bellum South* (New York: Oxford University Press, 1972), pp. 1–9; Winthrop D. Jordan, *White Over Black: American Attitudes toward the Negro, 1550–1812* (Chapel Hill: University of North Carolina Press, 1968), pp. 56–66, 84–85; James A. Padgett, "The Status of Slaves in Colonial North Carolina," *Journal of Negro History* 16 (July 1929): 301–2; and Wood, *Black Majority*, pp. 43–46. Herbert Aptheker, "Maroons within the Present Limits of the United States," in Richard Price, ed., *Maroon Societies: Rebel Slave Communities in the Americas* (New York: Doubleday, Anchor, 1973), p. 152; Brinn, "Blacks in Colonial North Carolina," pp. 105–6, 110; and William L. Saunders, ed., *The Colonial Records of North Carolina*, 10 vols. (Raleigh: State of North Carolina, 1886–90), 1:514, deal with runaways. Dena J. Epstein, *Sinful Tunes and Spirituals: Black Folk Music to the Civil War* (Urbana: University of Illinois Press, 1977), pp. 21–25, 30–38; and Ira De A. Reid, "The John Canoe Festival," *Phylon* 3 (Fourth Quarter 1942): 350–51, 357–60, treat African retentions.

30. Wood, *Black Majority*, esp. pp. 95–191.

31. Wesley Frank Craven, *White, Red, and Black: The Seventeenth-Century Virginian* (Charlottesville: University Press of Virginia, 1971); and Gary B. Nash, *Red, White, and Black: The Peoples of Early America* (Englewood Cliffs, N.J.: Prentice-Hall, 1974), examine multiracial interaction.

32. To be consulted, among others, are Saunders, ed., *Colonial Records*, vol. 1; and Parker et al., eds., *Colonial Records, Second Series*, vols. 2–3.

33. See Mitchell, *Records Relating to Blacks*, pp. 1, 3–4.

34. T. H. Breen and Stephen Innes, *"Myne Owne Ground": Race and Freedom on Virginia's Eastern Shore, 1640–1676* (New York: Oxford University Press, 1980).

35. The Englishman is quoted in Saunders, ed., *Colonial Records*, 1:527; and the Virginia governor in Morgan, *American Slavery—American Freedom*, p. 239.

36. Charles M. Andrews, *The Colonial Period of American History*, 4 vols. (New Haven: Yale University Press, 1934–38), vol. 3, *The Settlements*, pp. 246–50; and Wesley Frank Craven, *The Colonies in Transition, 1670–1713* (New York: Harper, 1968), p. 157, summarize contemporary views of North Carolina.

37. Bassett, *Slavery and Servitude*, p. 12. W. E. Burghardt Du Bois, *The Suppression of the African Slave Trade to the United States of America, 1638–1870* (New York: Longmans, 1896), differed on the African. He states, pp. 5–6, "In colonies like those in the West Indies and in South Carolina and Georgia, the rapid importation into America of a multitude of savages gave rise to a system of slavery far different from that which the late Civil War abolished. The strikingly harsh and even inhuman codes in these colonies show this. Crucifixion, burning, and starvation were legal modes of punishment. The rough and brutal character of the time and place was partly responsible for this, but a more decisive reason lay in the fierce and turbulent character of the imported Negroes."

38. Bassett, *Slavery and Servitude*, pp. 19–22, 23–26, 27–32.

39. The best example is Marvin L. Michael Kay and Lorin Lee Cary, "A Demographic Analysis of Colonial North Carolina with Special Emphasis upon the Slave and Black Populations," a paper delivered in Raleigh, North Carolina, 13 February 1981 and published in this volume. The authors demonstrate that Africans made up a third or more of the population in five of the colony's seven geographical regions, where they influenced cultural as well as legal patterns.

40. Cf. Bassett, *Slavery and Servitude*, pp. 19–22; Rosser Howard Taylor, *Slaveholding in North Carolina: An Economic View* (Chapel Hill: University of North Carolina Press, 1926), pp. 17–19; Guion Griffis Johnson, *Ante-Bellum North Carolina: A Social History* (Chapel Hill: University of North Carolina Press, 1937), pp. 8–12; Franklin, *Free Negro*, pp. 8–9; Jordan, *White Over Black*, pp. 102–3; and Crow, *Black Experience*, pp. 4–5.

41. See Harry Roy Merrens, *Colonial North Carolina in the Eighteenth Century: A Study in Historical Geography* (Chapel Hill: Univer-

sity of North Carolina Press, 1964), pp. 74–81. He adds, p. 177, that "within the east there were certainly major variations from place to place. From north to south, this section embraced the most densely settled portion of the colony (north of Albemarle Sound), the emptiest area (between Albemarle and Pamlico Sounds), and the region within which the plantation unit of occupancy was most common (the lower Cape Fear). . . . Slavery was everywhere more important than in the west."

42. Kay and Cary, "A Demographic Analysis of Colonial North Carolina," pp. 1–3, and Table 1; Bureau of the Census, *Historical Statistics of the United States: Colonial Times to 1970* (Washington, D.C.: Government Printing Office, 1975), p. 1168; Crow, *Black Experience*, p. 4; Franklin, *Free Negro*, p. 18. The figures are fragmentary at best. See Robert V. Wells, *The Population of the British Colonies in America before 1776: A Survey of Census Data* (Princeton: Princeton University Press, 1975), pp. 166–67.

43. Cf. Wood, "Study of Early Black History," p. 205; and Taylor, *Slaveholding*, pp. 20–21. Also, consult Philip D. Curtin, *The Atlantic Slave Trade: A Census* (Madison: University of Wisconsin Press, 1969), p. 158; and Elizabeth Donnan, ed., *Documents Illustrative of the History of the Slave Trade to America*, 4 vols. (Washington, D.C.: Carnegie Institution, 1930–35), vol. 4, *The Border Colonies and the Southern Colonies*, pp. v, 90, 235–36, 376, 415, 483.

44. Contrast Kay and Cary, "A Demographic Analysis of Colonial North Carolina," pp. 4–7, with Bassett, *Slavery and Servitude*, pp. 22–23; and Merrens, *Colonial North Carolina*, pp. 79–80, 226 (n. 61).

45. Kenneth W. Porter, "Negroes on the Southern Frontier, 1670–1763," *Journal of Negro History* 33 (January 1948): 53–78.

46. Among the most interesting are Daniel H. Usner, Jr., "Frontier Exchange in the Lower Mississippi Valley: Race Relations and Economic Life in Colonial Louisiana, 1699–1783," Ph.D. diss., Duke University, 1981; and William S. Willis, "Divide and Rule: Red, White, and Black in the Southeast," *Journal of Negro History* 48 (July 1963): 157–76, which covers South Carolina.

47. John Brickell, *The Natural History of North Carolina* (Dublin: Printed by James Carson, 1737), p. 273.

48. Theda Purdue, *Slavery and the Evolution of Cherokee Society, 1540–1866* (Knoxville: University of Tennessee Press, 1979), pp. iii–v, and passim. Cf. R. Halliburton, Jr., *Red Over Black: Black Slavery among the Cherokee Indians* (Westport, Conn.: Greenwood, 1977).

49. Cultural sharing is discussed in Wood, *Black Majority*, pp. 114–19; and *Paths toward Freedom*, pp. 16–18, 19–20, 25–27.

50. Bassett, *Slavery and Servitude*, pp. 14–16; Merrens, *Colonial North Carolina*, pp. 85–141.

51. A solid study of slave laws is Ernest James Clark, Jr., "Aspects of the North Carolina Slave Code, 1715–1860," *North Carolina Historical Review* 39 (April 1962): 148–64. Also, check Bassett, *Slavery and Servitude*, pp. 27–44; James K. Turner, "Slavery in Edgecombe County," in *Historical Papers*, ser. 12 (Durham: Trinity College Historical Society, 1916), pp. 5–36; Padgett, "Status of Slaves," pp. 303–27; Johnson, *Ante-Bellum North Carolina*, pp. 497–510; and Crow, *Black Experience*, pp. 19–33.

52. Marvin L. Michael Kay and Lorin Lee Cary, " 'The Planters Suffer Little or Nothing': North Carolina Compensations for Executed Slaves, 1748–1772," *Science and Society* 10 (Fall 1976): 288–306. Of interest, too, are Rosser H. Taylor, "Humanizing the Slave Code in North Carolina," *North Carolina Historical Review* 2 (July 1925): 324–25; and Jordan, *White Over Black*, pp. 154–58.

53. A. Leon Higginbotham, Jr., *In the Matter of Color: Race and the American Legal Process: The Colonial Period* (New York: Oxford University Press, 1978), pp. ix, 8–9, 153, and passim.

54. These findings are in Don Higginbotham and William S. Price, Jr., "Was It Murder for a White Man to Kill a Slave? Chief Justice Martin Howard Condemns the Peculiar Institution in North Carolina," *William and Mary Quarterly*, 3d ser., 36 (October 1979): 592–601; Clark, "North Carolina Slave Code," pp. 162–64; Helen T. Catterall, *Judicial Cases Concerning American Slavery and the Negro*, 5 vols. (Washington, D.C.: Carnegie Institution, 1926–37), vol. 2, *Cases from the Courts of North Carolina, South Carolina, and Tennessee*, pp. 1–15; and James Howard Brewer, "Legislation Designed to Control Slavery in Wilmington and Fayetteville," *North Carolina Historical Review* 30 (April 1953): 155–66. Cf. Franklin, *Free Negro*, pp. 58–61, 81–85; and Donald R. Lennon and Ida Brooks Kellam, eds. *The Wilmington Town Book, 1743–1778* (Raleigh: Department of Cultural Resources, 1973), pp. xxvii, xxx–xxxi, 18, 164–71, 197, 204–5.

55. In preparation is a study of slavery in North Carolina, 1748–72, to be published by the University of Illinois Press.

56. See Wilbon Harrison Daniel, "North Carolina Moravians and the Negro, 1760–1820," *Virginia Social Science Journal* 12 (April 1977): 23–31; William Herman Gehrke, "Negro Slavery among the Germans in North Carolina," *North Carolina Historical Review* 14 (October 1937): 307–24; Edward W. Phifer, "Slavery in Microcosm: Burke County, North Carolina," *Journal of Southern History* 28 (May 1962):

141–43; and Philip Africa, "Slaveholding in the Salem Community, 1771–1851," *North Carolina Historical Review* 54 (July 1977): 271, 275, and passim.

57. Peter Kent Opper, "North Carolina Quakers: Reluctant Slaveholders," *North Carolina Historical Review* 52 (January 1975): 37–43. Cf. William Edward Farrison, "The Negro Population of Guilford County, North Carolina, before the Civil War," *North Carolina Historical Review* 21 (October 1944): 319–29; and Hiram Horace Hilty, "North Carolina Quakers and Slavery," Ph.D. diss., Duke University, 1969.

58. Peter H. Wood, "'Jesus Christ Has Got Thee at Last': Afro-American Conversion as a Forgotten Chapter in Eighteenth-Century Southern Intellectual History," *Bulletin of the Center for the Study of Southern Culture and Religion* 3 (November 1979): 5, 6–7. Cf. Thomas W. Yonker, "The Negro Church in North Carolina, 1700–1900," M.A. thesis, Duke University, 1955.

59. Turner, "Slavery in Edgecombe County," pp. 25, 34. Also, see Marvin L. Michael Kay and Lorin Lee Cary, "Class, Mobility, and Conflict in North Carolina on the Eve of the Revolution," in Jeffrey J. Crow and Larry E. Tise, eds., *The Southern Experience in the American Revolution* (Chapel Hill: University of North Carolina Press, 1978), pp. 109, 119, 127, 129, 134, 145–46; Alan D. Watson, "Society and Economy in Colonial Edgecombe County," *North Carolina Historical Review* 50 (July 1973): 231, 247–48; and his *Society in Colonial North Carolina* (Raleigh: Department of Cultural Resources, 1975), pp. 8–10, 32.

60. Brickell, *Natural History*, p. 272; Janet Schaw, *Journal of a Lady of Quality*, ed. Evangeline Walker Andrews and Charles McLean Andrews (New Haven: Yale University Press, 1923), p. 177. Compare the impressions and racial views of Scotus Americanus, "Informations Concerning the Province of North Carolina, Etc. (1773)," in William K. Boyd, ed., *Some Eighteenth-Century Tracts Concerning North Carolina* (Raleigh: Edwards and Broughton, 1927), pp. 429–51; William Bartram, *Travels through North and South Carolina, Georgia, East and West Florida, the Cherokee Country* (Philadelphia: Printed by James and Johnson, 1791); William Attmore, *Journal of a Tour to North Carolina by William Attmore, 1787*, ed. Lida T. Rodman (Chapel Hill: University of North Carolina Press, 1922); Johann David Schoepf, *Travels in the Confederation, 1783–1784*, ed. and trans. Alfred J. Morrison (Philadelphia: W. J. Campbell, 1911); J. F. D. Smyth, *A Tour in the*

United States of America (Dublin: Price, Moncrieffe, 1784); and Elkanah Watson, *Men and Times of the Revolution: or, Memoirs of Elkanah Watson*, ed. Winslow C. Watson (New York: Dana and Co., 1856).

61. Philip D. Curtin, ed., *Africa Remembered: Narratives by West Africans from the Era of the Slave Trade* (Madison: University of Wisconsin Press, 1968), pp. 34–59, 69–98.

62. See Sidney Kaplan, *The Black Presence in the Era of the American Revolution, 1770–1800* (Washington, D.C.: Smithsonian Institution, 1973), esp. pp. 99–102, 231–35.

63. Quoted in ibid., p. 234.

64. Ira Berlin, "The Revolution in Black Life," in Alfred F. Young, ed., *The American Revolution: Explorations in the History of American Radicalism* (DeKalb: Northern Illinois University Press, 1976), p. 362.

65. Crow, *Black Experience*, esp. pp. 34–63, 97–103. Also, consider Lindley S. Butler, *North Carolina and the Coming of the Revolution, 1763–1776* (Raleigh: Department of Cultural Resources, 1976), p. 59; Robert M. Calhoon, *Religion and the American Revolution in North Carolina* (Raleigh: Department of Cultural Resources, 1976), pp. 66–68; Alice E. Mathews, *Society in Revolutionary North Carolina* (Raleigh: Department of Cultural Resources, 1976), pp. 7–8, 63–67; and Carole Watterson Troxler, *The Loyalist Experience in North Carolina* (Raleigh: Department of Cultural Resources, 1976), pp. 49–54.

66. Crow, "Slave Rebelliousness and Social Conflict in North Carolina, 1775 to 1802," *William and Mary Quarterly*, 3d ser., 37 (January 1980): 79–102. Complementing the latter is Alan D. Watson, "Impulse toward Independence: Resistance and Rebellion among North Carolina Slaves, 1750–1775," *Journal of Negro History* 63 (Fall 1978): 317–28.

67. Cf. Franklin, *Free Negro*, pp. 58–61, 121–23; and Herbert G. Gutman, *The Black Family in Slavery and Freedom, 1750–1925* (New York: Pantheon, 1976), pp. 169–84.

68. Bassett, *Slavery in the State*, pp. 7, 10–28; Johnson, *Ante-Bellum North Carolina*, pp. 468, 510-59.

69. Compare Yasuko Ichihashi Shinoda, "Lands and Slaves in North Carolina in 1860," Ph.D. diss., University of North Carolina at Chapel Hill, 1971, with Ralph V. Anderson, "Labor Utilization and Productivity, Diversification, and Self-Sufficiency: Southern Plantations, 1800–1840," Ph.D. diss., University of North Carolina at Chapel Hill, 1974; William Kauffman Scarborough, "Plantation Management in the Ante-Bellum South: The Overseer," Ph.D. diss., University of North Caro-

lina at Chapel Hill, 1961; and Robert William Fogel and Stanley L. Engerman, *Time on the Cross: The Economics of American Negro Slavery* (Boston: Little, Brown, 1974).

70. James H. Boykin, *The Negro in North Carolina prior to 1861: An Historical Monograph* (New York: Pageant Press, 1958); James H. Brewer, "An Account of Negro Slavery in the Cape Fear prior to 1860," Ph.D. diss., University of Pittsburgh, 1949.

71. Bassett, *Slavery in the State*, p. 33.

72. For Tar Heel proslavery thinkers, consult William Sumner Jenkins, *Pro-Slavery Thought in the Old South* (Chapel Hill: University of North Carolina Press, 1935); and Larry Edward Tise, "Proslavery Ideology: A Social and Intellectual History of the Defense of Slavery in America, 1790–1840," Ph.D. diss., University of North Carolina at Chapel Hill, 1974. Monty Woodall Cox, "Freedom during the Frémont Campaign: The Fate of One North Carolina Republican in 1856," *North Carolina Historical Review* 45 (October 1968): 357–83; Victor B. Howard, "John Brown's Raid at Harpers Ferry and the Sectional Crisis in North Carolina," *North Carolina Historical Review* 55 (October 1978): 396–420; and Clement Eaton, *The Freedom-of-Thought Struggle in the Old South*, rev. enl. (New York: Harper, 1964), cover the persecution of antislavery dissenters.

73. See Bryce R. Holt, "The Supreme Court of North Carolina and Slavery," M.A. thesis, Duke University, 1924; Ernest James Clark, "Slave Cases before the North Carolina Supreme Court, 1818–1858," M.A. thesis, University of North Carolina at Chapel Hill, 1959; and Patrick S. Brady, "Slavery, Race, and the Criminal Law in Antebellum North Carolina: A Reconsideration of the Thomas Ruffin Court," *North Carolina Central Law Journal* 10 (Spring 1979): 248–60.

74. Cf. Donald C. Butts, "A Challenge to Planter Rule: The Controversy over the Ad Valorem Taxation of Slaves in North Carolina, 1858–1862," Ph.D. diss., Duke University, 1978; and the case against Tar Heel planters in Hinton Rowan Helper, *The Impending Crisis of the South: How to Meet It* (New York: Burdick Brothers, 1857).

75. North Carolina colonizationists are discussed by Memory F. Mitchell, "Off to Africa—with Judicial Blessing," *North Carolina Historical Review* 53 (Summer 1976): 265–87; Peter Kent Opper, "'Old Jane Seems to Be a Coming Too': A History of the Migration, Emigration, and Colonization of the North Carolina Negro, 1816–1835," M.A. thesis, University of North Carolina at Chapel Hill, 1969; Thomas C. Parramore, "A Passage to Monrovia," paper delivered to the 1973 North Carolina Social Science Faculties meeting at Chowan College,

Murfreesboro, North Carolina; and Patrick Sowle, "The North Carolina Manumission Society, 1816–1834," *North Carolina Historical Review* 42 (Winter 1965): 47–69. Moralists are profiled in Willie Grier Todd, "North Carolina Baptists and Slavery," *North Carolina Historical Review* 24 (April 1947): 135–59; Paul M. Ford, "Calvin H. Wiley's View of the Negro," *North Carolina Historical Review* 41 (Winter 1964): 1–20; and John B. Weaver, "Calvin Henderson Wiley and the Problem of Slavery, 1850–1865," M.A. thesis, University of North Carolina at Chapel Hill, 1975.

76. Carl N. Degler, *The Other South: Southern Dissenters in the Nineteenth Century* (New York: Harper, 1974); Charles Fitzgerald McKiever, *Slavery and the Emigration of North Carolina Friends* (Murfreesboro, N.C.: Johnson Publishing Co., 1970). For antislavery activities, including the Friends, see John Spencer Bassett, *Anti-Slavery Leaders of North Carolina* (Baltimore: Johns Hopkins Press, 1898); Clifton H. Johnson, "Abolitionist Missionary Activities," *North Carolina Historical Review* 40 (Summer 1963): 295–320; Linda D. Keys, "Some Aspects of Slavery in North Carolina," M.A. thesis, North Carolina Central University, 1975; Emma King, "Some Aspects of the Work of the Society of Friends for Negro Education in North Carolina," *North Carolina Historical Review* 1 (October 1924): 403–11; John Michael Shay, "The Anti-Slavery Movement in North Carolina," Ph.D. diss., Princeton University, 1971; and Noble J. Tolbert, "Daniel Worth: Tar Heel Abolitionist," *North Carolina Historical Review* 39 (Summer 1962): 284–304.

77. Phifer, "Burke County." Cf. Donnie D. Bellamy, "Slavery in Microcosm: Onslow County, North Carolina," *Journal of Negro History* 62 (October 1977): 339–50; Turner, "Slavery in Edgecombe County"; and Benjamin F. Callahan, "The North Carolina Slave Patrol," M.A. thesis, University of North Carolina at Chapel Hill, 1973.

78. See Blassingame, *Slave Community*; Eugene D. Genovese, *Roll, Jordan, Roll: The World the Slaves Made* (New York: Pantheon, 1974); Leslie Howard Owens, *This Species of Property: Slave Life and Culture in the Old South* (New York: Oxford University Press, 1976); and George P. Rawick, ed., *The American Slave: A Composite Autobiography*, ser. 1, 19 vols. (Westport, Conn.: Greenwood, 1972), vol. 1, *From Sundown to Sunup: The Making of the Black Community*.

79. However, a number of topics have been studied. See John Hope Franklin, "Slaves Virtually Free in Ante-Bellum North Carolina," *Journal of Negro History* 28 (July 1943): 248–310; C. W. Harper, "House Servants and Field Hands: Fragmentation in the Antebellum Slave Com-

munity," *North Carolina Historical Review* 55 (Winter 1978): 42–59; Shirley M. Jackson, "Black Slave Drivers in the Southern United States," Ph.D. diss., Bowling Green State University, 1977; Katherine Ann McGeachy, "The North Carolina Slave Code," M.A. thesis, University of North Carolina at Chapel Hill, 1948; Ralph Thomas Parkinson, "The Religious Instruction of Slaves, 1820–1860," M.A. thesis, University of North Carolina at Chapel Hill, 1948; Todd L. Savitt, "Slave Life Insurance in Virginia and North Carolina," *Journal of Southern History* 43 (November 1977): 585–600; and Susan Duncan Sides, "Women and Slaves: An Interpretation Based on the Writings of Southern Women," Ph.D. diss., University of North Carolina at Chapel Hill, 1969.

80. For examples, see Benjamin Quarles, *Black Abolitionists* (New York: Oxford University Press, 1969); Howard Holman Bell, ed., *Minutes of the Proceedings of the National Negro Conventions, 1830–1864* (New York: Arno Press and the New York Times, 1969); John W. Blassingame, ed., *Slave Testimony: Two Centuries of Letters, Speeches, Interviews, and Autobiographies* (Baton Rouge: Louisiana State University Press, 1977); Paul D. Escott, *Slavery Remembered: A Record of Twentieth-Century Slave Narratives* (Chapel Hill: University of North Carolina Press, 1979); and Rawick, ed., *American Slave*, vol. 14, *N. C. Narratives, Part 1*; vol. 15, *N. C. Narratives, Part 2*; and supple. ser. 1, 12 vols. (Westport, Conn.: Greenwood, 1977), vol. 11, *N. C. and S. C. Narratives*.

81. A preliminary report is Marguerite Schumann, "The Quarters at Horton Grove," *Tar Heel* (July 1980): 16, 71.

82. Rosser H. Taylor, "Slave Conspiracies in North Carolina," *North Carolina Historical Review* 5 (January 1928): 20–34.

83. Herbert Aptheker, *American Negro Slave Revolts* (New York: Columbia University Press, 1943). Cf. Robert N. Elliott, "The Nat Turner Insurrection as Reported in the North Carolina Press," *North Carolina Historical Review* 38 (January 1961): 1–18; and Dorris Lea Raper, "The Effects of David Walker's Appeal and Nat Turner's Insurrection on North Carolina," M.A. thesis, University of North Carolina at Chapel Hill, 1969.

84. Eddie Marie Ervin, "Runaway Slaves in Ante-Bellum North Carolina," M.A. thesis, North Carolina College, 1946.

85. Besides Ervin, cited above, Crow, "Slave Rebelliousness and Social Conflict," and Freddie Lee Parker, "Slave Protest in North Carolina, 1775–1835," M.A. thesis, North Carolina Central University, 1976, virtually no other titles have surfaced.

86. Franklin, *Free Negro*, pp. 163–91, and "The Free Negro in the Economic Life of Ante-Bellum North Carolina," *North Carolina Historical Review* 19 (July 1942): 239–59, (October 1942): 358–74. Also see Ira Berlin, *Slaves Without Masters: The Free Negro in the Antebellum South* (New York: Pantheon, 1974), pp. 92–99; James Blackwell Browning, "The Free Negro in Ante-Bellum North Carolina," *North Carolina Historical Review* 15 (January 1938): 23–33; Margaret Burr DesChamps, "John Chavis as a Preacher to Whites," *North Carolina Historical Review* 32 (April 1935): 165–72; and Rosser H. Taylor, "The Free Negro in North Carolina," M.A. thesis, University of North Carolina at Chapel Hill, 1920.

87. W. E. B. Du Bois, *Black Reconstruction in America, 1860–1880* (New York: Harcourt, Brace, 1935), p. 59.

88. Leon F. Litwack, *Been in the Storm So Long: The Aftermath of Slavery* (New York: Knopf, 1979), which encompasses black Tar Heels, has given it a boost.

89. Robert F. Durden, *The Gray and the Black: The Confederate Debate on Emancipation* (Baton Rouge: Louisiana State University Press, 1972), pp. 95, 176–81; and Paul D. Escott, *After Secession: Jefferson Davis and the Failure of Confederate Nationalism* (Baton Rouge: Louisiana State University, 1978), pp. 89, 96–97, 200–203, 205, 207. Cf. J. Allen Jernigan, "Making Soldiers of Slaves: Pat Cleburne, North Carolina, and the Price of Southern Independence," honors essay, University of North Carolina at Chapel Hill, 1980; Harold D. Moser, "Reaction in North Carolina to the Emancipation Proclamation," *North Carolina Historical Review* 44 (Winter 1967): 53–71.

90. James H. Brewer, *The Confederate Negro: Virginia's Craftsmen and Military Laborers, 1861–1865* (Durham: Duke University Press, 1969), esp. pp. 26, 49, 80, 85–88.

91. For examples, see Randall M. Miller, ed., "'It Is Good to Be Religious': A Loyal Slave on God, Masters, and the Civil War," *North Carolina Historical Review* 54 (January 1977): 66–71; and B. H. Nelson, "Some Aspects of Negro Life in North Carolina during the Civil War," *North Carolina Historical Review* 25 (April 1948): 143–66.

92. Cf. Tracy Whittaker Schneider, "The Institution of Slavery in North Carolina, 1860–1865," Ph.D. diss., Duke University, 1979; and W. Buck Yearns and John G. Barrett, eds., *North Carolina Civil War Documentary* (Chapel Hill: University of North Carolina Press, 1980), pp. 53–56, 147–8, 246–57, 254–61. For examples of black rebellion, read Beth G. Crabtree and James W. Patton, eds., *"Journal of a Secesh Lady": The Diary of Catherine Ann Devereux Edmondston, 1860–1866*

(Raleigh: Department of Cultural Resources, 1979), pp. 528–30, 533, 536.

93. Litwack, *Been in the Storm*, pp. 52, 465–66, 502–7; Schneider, "Institution of Slavery," pp. 165–68; Tinsley Lee Spraggins, "Mobilization of Negro Labor for the Department of Virginia and North Carolina, 1861–1865," *North Carolina Historical Review* 24 (April 1947): 160–97; and Hessie Severt Williams, "A Comparative Analysis of Ex-Slave Thoughts Concerning Their Masters, the United States Army, and Freedom," M.A. thesis, University of North Carolina at Chapel Hill, 1969.

94. For its scope, see Horace James, *Annual Report of the Superintendent of Negro Affairs in North Carolina, 1864* (Boston: W. F. Brown, 1865); and Yearns and Barrett, eds., *Civil War Documentary*, pp. 49–52.

95. Extremely anti-Negro is J. G. de Roulhac Hamilton, *Reconstruction in North Carolina* (New York: Columbia University Press, 1914).

96. Consider Elizabeth Balanoff, "Negro Legislators in the North Carolina General Assembly, July, 1868–February, 1872," *North Carolina Historical Review* 49 (January 1972): 22–55; Arthur DeMurro, "'We Are Men': Black Reconstruction in North Carolina, 1865–1870," M.A. thesis, University of North Carolina at Chapel Hill, 1979; Austin Marcus Drumm, "The Union League in the Carolinas," Ph.D. diss., University of North Carolina at Chapel Hill, 1955; W. McKee Evans, *Ballots and Fence Rails: Reconstruction on the Lower Cape Fear* (Chapel Hill: University of North Carolina Press, 1967); and Samuel Denny Smith, *The Negro in Congress, 1870–1901* (Chapel Hill: University of North Carolina Press, 1940).

97. Roberta Sue Alexander, "Hostility and Hope: Black Education in North Carolina during Presidential Reconstruction, 1865–1867," *North Carolina Historical Review* 53 (April 1976): 113–32; John L. Bell, Jr., "Baptists and the Negro in North Carolina during Reconstruction," *North Carolina Historical Review* 42 (October 1965): 391–409; George R. Bentley, *A History of the Freedmen's Bureau* (Philadelphia: University of Pennsylvania Press, 1955); James A. Padgett, "From Slavery to Prominence in North Carolina," *Journal of Negro History* 22 (October 1937): 433–87; and Robert Hayne Rivers, "The Relationship between White and Negro Baptists in the Churches of North Carolina from 1830–1870," M.A. thesis, Duke University, 1963.

98. Du Bois, *Black Reconstruction*, pp. 526–36; Murray, *Proud Shoes*, pp. 214–40.

99. Gutman, *Black Family*, pp. 363–431; George W. McDaniel, "Stagville: Kin and Community" (Stagville Preservation Center, September 1977); Jacqueline Baldwin Walker, "Blacks in North Carolina during Reconstruction," Ph.D. diss., Duke University, 1979. Of interest, too, is that both Charles L. Price of East Carolina University and Stephen F. Reilly, a Duke graduate student, are preparing studies of the North Carolina Freedmen's Bureau.

100. These include Eric Anderson, *Race and Politics in North Carolina, 1872–1901: The Black Second* (Baton Rouge: Louisiana State University Press, 1981); Dorothy Hawkins Bryan, "The Political Career of George Henry White, North Carolinian, 1880–1901," M.A. thesis, North Carolina College, 1963; John Timothy Byrd, "The Disfranchisement of Blacks in New Hanover County, North Carolina," M.A. thesis, University of North Carolina at Chapel Hill, 1976; Jerry Wayne Cotten, "Negro Disfranchisement in North Carolina: The Politics of Race in a Southern State," M.A. thesis, University of North Carolina at Chapel Hill, 1973; Jeffrey J. Crow, "'Fusion, Confusion, and Negroism': Schisms among Negro Republicans in the North Carolina Election of 1896," *North Carolina Historical Review* 53 (October 1976): 364–84; Helen G. Edmonds, *The Negro and Fusion Politics in North Carolina, 1894–1901* (Chapel Hill: University of North Carolina Press, 1951); Joseph Elliot Elmore, "North Carolina Negro Congressmen, 1875–1901," M.A. thesis, University of North Carolina at Chapel Hill, 1965; John Emory Fleming, "Out of Bondage: The Adjustment of Burke County Negroes after the Civil War, 1865–1890," Ph.D. diss., Howard University, 1974; J. Morgan Kousser, *The Shaping of Southern Politics: Suffrage Restriction and the Establishment of the One-Party South* (New Haven: Yale University Press, 1974); William Alexander Mabry, "'White Supremacy' and the North Carolina Suffrage Amendment," *North Carolina Historical Review* 13 (January 1936): 1–24; Jerome A. McDuffie, "Politics in Wilmington and New Hanover County, North Carolina, 1865–1900: The Genesis of a Race Riot," Ph.D. diss., Kent State University, 1979; H. Leon Prather, "The Red Shirt Movement in North Carolina, 1898–1900," *Journal of Negro History* 62 (April 1977): 174–84; Howard N. Rabinowitz, *Race Relations in the Urban South, 1865–1890* (New York: Oxford University Press, 1978); George W. Reid, "A Biography of George H. White, 1852–1918," Ph.D. diss., Howard University, 1974; Errol Henry Stambler, "The Struggle over Disfranchisement in North Carolina, 1898–1910," M.A. thesis, University of North Carolina at Chapel Hill, 1972; and Allen W. Trelease,

"The Fusion Legislatures of 1895 and 1897: A Roll-Call Analysis of the North Carolina House of Representatives," *North Carolina Historical Review* 57 (July 1980): 208–309.

101. See, for example, his book *The Negro in North Carolina, 1876–1894* (Chapel Hill: University of North Carolina Press, 1964); and his articles "Factors Influencing the Efficiency of Negro Farm Laborers in Post-Reconstruction North Carolina," *Agricultural History* 33 (October 1959): 185–89; "The Colored Industrial Association of North Carolina and Its Fair of 1886," *North Carolina Historical Review* 34 (January 1957): 58–67; "The Economic Status of the Town Negro in Post-Reconstruction North Carolina," *North Carolina Historical Review* 35 (October 1958): 448–60; "Legal Status of Public School Education for Negroes in North Carolina, 1877–1894," *North Carolina Historical Review* 32 (July 1955): 346–57; "The Movement in North Carolina to Establish a State-Supported College for Negroes," *North Carolina Historical Review* 35 (April 1958): 45–65; and "The Movement of Negroes from North Carolina, 1876–1894," *North Carolina Historical Review* 33 (January 1956): 45–65.

102. Allen Edward Burgess, "Tar Heel Blacks and the New South Dream: The Coleman Manufacturing Company, 1896–1904," Ph.D. diss., Duke University, 1977; I. Garland Penn, *The Afro-American Press and Its Editors* (Springfield, Mass.: Wiley, 1891).

103. Marjorie Applewhite, "Sharecropper and Tenant in the Courts of North Carolina," *North Carolina Historical Review* 31 (April 1954): 134–49; John Richard Dennett, *The South as It Is, 1865–1866*, ed. Henry W. Christman (New York: Viking, 1965), esp. pp. 108–11, 119, 125, 128; Rebecca Scott, "The Battle over the Child: Child Apprenticeship and the Freedmen's Bureau in North Carolina," *Prologue* 10 (Summer 1978): 101–12.

104. Richard Barry Westin, "The State and Segregated Schools: Negro Public Education in North Carolina, 1863–1923," Ph.D. diss., Duke University, 1966; Linda Claudette Wright, "Black Durham, 1870–1898," M.A. paper, Duke University, 1976.

105. See Sydney Nathans, "Fortress without Walls: A Black Community, 1840–1970," in Carol B. Stack and Robert L. Hall, eds., *Holding on to the Land and the Lord* (Athens: University of Georgia Press, 1982). But also see Nell Irvin Painter, *Exodusters: Black Migration to Kansas after Reconstruction* (New York: Knopf, 1977); and Joseph H. Taylor, "The Great Migration from North Carolina in 1879," *North Carolina Historical Review* 31 (January 1954): 18–33.

106. Willard B. Gatewood, "North Carolina's Negro Regiment in the Spanish-American War," *North Carolina Historical Review* 48 (Autumn 1971): 370–87; Dorothy A. Gay, "Crisis of Identity: The Negro Community in Raleigh, 1890–1900," *North Carolina Historical Review* 50 (April 1973): 121–40; Melton McLaurin, "The Knights of Labor in North Carolina Politics," *North Carolina Historical Review* 49 (July 1972): 298–315.

107. Joseph B. Bethea, "Black Methodists in North Carolina," in O. Kelly Ingram, ed., *Methodism Alive in North Carolina* (Durham: Duke Divinity School, 1976), pp. 87–97; J. W. Hood, *One Hundred Years of the African Methodist Episcopal Zion Church* (New York: A.M.E. Zion Book Concern, 1895); Elwynn Webster Midgett, "Negro Baptists in North Carolina, 1865–1900," M.A. thesis, North Carolina College, 1949; J. A. Whitted, *A History of Negro Baptists of North Carolina* (Raleigh: Edwards and Broughton, 1908).

108. Sydney Nathans, *The Quest for Progress: The Way We Lived in North Carolina, 1870–1920* (Chapel Hill: University of North Carolina Press, 1983); see especially his chapter titled "From Jubilee to Jim Crow."

109. Cf. Logan, "Movement of Negroes," and Taylor, "Great Migration in 1879."

110. The building blocks for the analysis are in C. Eric Lincoln, "Black Religion in North Carolina: From Colonial Times to 1900," in Crow and Winters, eds., *Black Presence*, pp. 9–24.

111. See W. H. Quick, *Negro Stars in All Ages of the World* (Richmond: Adkins, 1898); William J. Simmons, *Men of Mark: Eminent, Progressive, and Rising* (Cleveland: G. M. Rewell, 1887); and William Jacob Walls, *Joseph Charles Price: Educator and Race Leader* (Boston: Christopher Publishing House, 1943).

112. John H. Haley III, "The Carolina Chameleon: Charles N. Hunter and Race Relations in North Carolina, 1865–1931," Ph.D. diss., University of North Carolina at Chapel Hill, 1981. Graphically illustrated is Louise Daniel Hutchinson, *Anna J. Cooper: A Voice from the South* (Washington, D.C.: Smithsonian Institution, 1981). Cf. Hunter, "Charlotte Hawkins Brown"; and Flora Hatley, "Anna Julia Haywood Cooper: Educator-Women's Rights Activist," M.A. thesis, North Carolina Central University, 1980.

113. Roland C. McConnell, *The Negro in North Carolina since Reconstruction: An Abridgment* (New York: New York University, 1949); Lawrence A. Oxley, *The North Carolina Negro* (n.p.: Printed by au-

thority of the State of Illinois, 1927); and Federal Writers' Project, *North Carolina: A Guide to the Old North State* (Chapel Hill: University of North Carolina Press, 1939), pp. 51–57.

114. Weare, *Black Business*. Cf. Abram L. Harris, *The Negro as Capitalist: A Study of Banking and Business among American Negroes* (Philadelphia: American Academy of Political and Social Science, 1936); and Kennedy, *Mutual Story*.

115. Wade Hamilton Boggs III, "State-Supported Higher Education for Blacks in North Carolina, 1877–1945," Ph.D. diss., Duke University, 1972; Louis R. Harlan, *Separate and Unequal: Public School Campaigns and Racism in the Southern Seaboard States, 1901–1915* (Chapel Hill: University of North Carolina Press, 1958); Westin, "The State and Segregated Schools."

116. For a sampling of works on black colleges, see Hugh V. Brown, *A History of the Education of Negroes in North Carolina* (Raleigh: Irving-Swain Press, 1961); Wilmoth A. Carter, *Shaw's Universe: A Monument to Educational Innovation* (Raleigh: Shaw University, 1973); Alfonso Elder, *Freshmen and Seniors in the Negro Colleges in North Carolina* (Durham: North Carolina College, 1927); Warmoth R. Gibbs, *History of the North Carolina Agricultural and Technical College* (Dubuque, Iowa: William C. Brown, 1966); Cecil D. Halliburton, *A History of St. Augustine's College, 1867–1937* (Raleigh: St. Augustine's College, 1937); Clara Barnes Jenkins, "An Historical Study of Shaw University, 1865–1963," Ed.D. diss., University of Pittsburgh, 1965; Evelyn Adelaide Johnson, *History of Elizabeth City State University: A Story of Survival* (New York: Vantage Press, 1980); Mildred P. Jones, *History of Fayetteville State College* (Fayetteville: State College, 1969); Rudolph Jones, "The Development of Negro State Colleges and Normal Schools in North Carolina," *Quarterly Review of Higher Education among Negroes* 5 (April 1938): 132–44; Ella Louise Murphy, "Origin and Development of Fayetteville State Teachers College, 1867–1959: A Chapter in the History of the Education of Negroes in North Carolina," Ph.D. diss., New York University, 1960; N. C. Newbold, *Five North Carolina Negro Educators* (Chapel Hill: University of North Carolina Press, 1939). Frequently, autobiographies provide the best insights into black education during the segregation era. See Rose Butler Browne and James W. English, *Love My Children: An Autobiography* (New York: Meredith Press, 1969); and Mary E. Mebane, *Mary* (New York: Viking, 1981).

117. All the following are by English professors and folklorists:

Bruce Bastin, "Black Music in North Carolina," in Crow and Winters, eds., *Black Presence*, pp. 41–52; J. Mason Brewer, *Worser Days and Better Times: The Folklore of the North Carolina Negro* (Chicago: Quadrangle, 1965); Portia Naomi Crawford, "A Study of Negro Folk Songs from Greensboro, North Carolina, and Surrounding Towns," M.A. thesis, University of North Carolina at Chapel Hill, 1966; Blyden Jackson, "Black Literature in North Carolina," in Crow and Winters, eds., *Black Presence*, pp. 25–39; and Walser, *Literary North Carolina*. See also Richard Walser, "His Worship The John Kuner," *North Carolina Folklore Journal* 19 (November 1971): 160–72; and Clyde R. Appleton, "Singing in the Streets of Raleigh, 1963: Some Recollections," *Black Perspective in Music* 3 (Fall 1975): 243–52.

118. See John R. Larkins, *The Negro Population of North Carolina: Social and Economic* (Raleigh: Department of Public Welfare, 1944). Urban migration stimulated the development of all-black institutions. For an example, cf. William T. Grimes, "The History of Kate Bitting Reynolds Memorial Hospital," *Journal of the National Medical Association* 64 (July 1972): 376–81; and Robert W. Prichard, "Winston-Salem's Black Hospitals Prior to 1930," *Journal of the National Medical Association* 68 (May 1976): 246–49.

119. Useful are tapes and transcripts of the Oral History Interviews, Winston-Salem State University, and those in the Southern Oral History Project, University of North Carolina, which Allen Tullos is culling for a study of black and white industrial workers. Cf. Delores Elizabeth Janiewski, "From Field to Factory: Race, Class, Sex, and the Woman Worker in Durham, 1880–1940," Ph.D. diss., Duke University, 1979.

120. Ralph J. Bunche, *The Political Status of the Negro in the Age of FDR*, ed. Dewey W. Grantham (Chicago: University of Chicago Press, 1973); Robert Cannon, "The Organization and Growth of Black Political Participation in Durham, North Carolina, 1933–1958," Ph.D. diss., University of North Carolina at Chapel Hill, 1975; Key, *Southern Politics*; William A. Mabry, *The Negro in North Carolina Politics since Reconstruction* (Durham: Duke University Press, 1940).

121. See Linda D. Addo and James H. McCallum, *To Be Faithful to Our Heritage: A History of Black United Methodism in North Carolina* (Winston-Salem: Hunter Publishing Co., 1930); Agnes Brown, "The Negro Churches of Chapel Hill: A Community Study," M.A. thesis, University of North Carolina at Chapel Hill, 1939; Ralph A. Felton, *Go Down Moses: A Study of Twenty-one Successful Rural Pastors* (Madison, N.J.: Department of the Rural Church, Drew Theological Semi-

nary, 1952). The Black Church Project at Duke University, headed by
C. Eric Lincoln, is collecting data nationally. Its North Carolina material should be most helpful.

122. Burns, "North Carolina and the Negro Dilemma"; Gaines M.
Foster, "Bishop Cheshire and Black Participation in the Episcopal
Church: The Limitations of Religious Paternalism," *North Carolina
Historical Review* 54 (Winter 1977): 49–65; Thomas H. Houck, "A
Newspaper History of Race Relations in Durham, North Carolina,
1910–1940," M.A. thesis, Duke University, 1941; William E. King,
"Charles McIver Fights for the Tar Heel Negro's Right to an Educa-
tion," *North Carolina Historical Review* 41 (July 1964): 360–69; John
H. Stevenson, "The Attitude of the Raleigh *News and Observer* toward
the Negro, 1944–1945," M.A. thesis, Howard University, 1948.

123. Of numerous titles, see Augustus M. Burns III, "Graduate Edu-
cation for Blacks in North Carolina, 1930–1951," *Journal of Southern
History* 45 (May 1980): 195–218; J. Morgan Kousser, "Progressivism
for Middle Class Whites Only: North Carolina Education, 1880–1910,"
Journal of Southern History 46 (May 1980): 169–94; Charles S. John-
son, *Patterns of Negro Segregation* (New York: Harper, 1943); Pauli
Murray, comp. and ed., *States' Laws on Race and Color* (New York:
Woman's Division of the Methodist Church, 1951); *Thirty Years of
Lynching in the United States, 1889–1918* (New York: National Asso-
ciation for the Advancement of Colored People, 1919); and Archer
Rudder Turner, "The Development of Statutory Racial Segregation in
North Carolina since 1890," B.D. thesis, Duke University Divinity
School, 1945.

124. William J. Breen, "Black Women and the Great War: Mobiliza-
tion and Reform in the South," *Journal of Southern History* 44 (August
1974): 421–40; Hugh P. Brinton, "The Negro in Durham," Ph.D. diss.,
University of North Carolina, 1930; Constance Hill Marteena, comp.,
Achievements of Afro-American Women of the Twentieth Century
(Greensboro: Negro Library Association, 1949); Nathan Alvin Pitts,
The Cooperative Movement in Negro Communities of North Carolina
(Washington, D.C.: Catholic University of America Press, 1950); Don-
ald W. Wyatt, "Negro Youth in Greensboro, North Carolina," *In Thus
Be Their Destiny: The Personality Development of Negro Youth in Three
Communities* (Washington, D.C.: American Council on Education,
1941); and Bertha H. Miller, "Blacks in Winston-Salem, North Caro-
lina, 1895–1920: Community Development in an Era of Benevolent Paternalism," Ph.D. diss., Duke University, 1981.

125. Cf. Charles S. Johnson, *To Stem This Tide: A Survey of Racial*

Tension Areas in the United States (Boston: Pilgrim Press, 1943); and Howard W. Odum, *Race and Rumors of Race: Challenge to American Crisis* (Chapel Hill: University of North Carolina Press, 1943).

126. Chafe, *Civilities and Civil Rights*, pp. 1–2 ff.

127. Barksdale, "The Indigenous Civil Rights Movement"; and Aingred Ghislayne Dunston, "The Black Struggle for Equality in Winston-Salem, North Carolina, 1947–1977," Ph.D. diss., Duke University, 1981.

128. M. Elaine Burgess, *Negro Leadership in a Southern City* (Chapel Hill: University of North Carolina Press, 1960); Everett Carl Ladd, Jr., *Negro Political Leadership in the South* (Ithaca: Cornell University Press, 1966); John R. Larkins, *Patterns of Leadership among Negroes in North Carolina* (Raleigh: Irving-Swain Press, 1959); Arthur M. Miller, "Desegregation and Negro Leadership in Durham, North Carolina, 1954–1963," M.A. thesis, University of North Carolina at Chapel Hill, 1976; Bradbury Seasholes, "Negro Political Participation in Two North Carolina Cities," Ph.D. diss., University of North Carolina at Chapel Hill, 1962.

129. See Akosua Barthwell, *Trade Unionism in North Carolina: The Strike Against Reynolds Tobacco, 1947* (New York: American Institute of Marxist Studies, 1977); Earl R. Edwards, "North Carolina's Reaction to the Supreme Court Decisions on Public School Segregation," M.A. thesis, North Carolina College, 1959; Ehle, *Free Men*; Melvin L. Murphy, "The Harriett-Henderson Textile Mill Strike, 1958," M.A. thesis, North Carolina Central University, 1965; Truman Nelson, *People with Strength in Monroe, North Carolina* (New York: Committee to Aid the Monroe Defendants, 1963); Robert F. Williams, *Negroes with Guns* (New York: Marzani and Munsell, 1962); and Wolff, *Lunch at the Five and Ten*.

130. Jesse Lee Allen, "The Effects of School Desegregation on the Employment Status of Negro Principals in North Carolina," Ed.D. diss., Duke University, 1969; A. B. Cochran III, "School Desegregation in North Carolina: Dimensions of a Public Policy," Ph.D. diss., University of North Carolina at Chapel Hill, 1972; William Henry Coogan III, "School Board Decisions on Desegregation in North Carolina," Ph.D. diss., University of North Carolina at Chapel Hill, 1971; Richard Anthony Lamanna, "The Negro Public School Teacher and School Desegregation: A Survey of Negro Teachers in North Carolina," Ph.D. diss., University of North Carolina at Chapel Hill, 1966; Dorothy Elizabeth Pittman, "Reactions to Desegregation: A Study of Negro Mothers," Ph.D. diss., University of North Carolina at Chapel Hill,

1959; Steven Francis Redburn, "Protest and Policy in Durham, North Carolina," Ph.D. diss., University of North Carolina at Chapel Hill, 1970.

131. For a general study of SNCC, see Clayborne Carson, *In Struggle: SNCC and the Black Awakening of the 1960s* (Cambridge: Harvard University Press, 1981). Also, see Mimi Conway, *Rise Gonna Rise: A Portrait of Southern Textile Workers* (Garden City, N.Y.: Doubleday, Anchor, 1979); Janiewski, "From Field to Factory"; Vernon Benjamin Kiser, "Occupational Change among Negroes in Durham," M.A. thesis, Duke University, 1942; and Wise, "Stirring the Pot."

132. Wood, "Study of Early Black History," p. 224.

2. History from the Hands of Black Americans

A Methodological Proposal

Leland Ferguson

There are two general techniques used to derive information about the past. The most common is direct communication with living informants. The other is to study things, or artifacts, that have survived from an earlier time. The first of these techniques has been labeled oral history and folklore by scholars, while the latter is divided into at least three fields of study: history, the study of curated written artifacts; folklife, the study of commonly used artifacts that have survived within our culture; and archaeology, the study of artifacts and other information that must be recovered from the ground.

Recent Archaeology

The archaeological study of black Americans is a fledgling study within the discipline of historical archaeology, which is little more than fledgling itself. Although there has been some minor archaeological study of the historic period since the middle of the nineteenth century, the serious study of historic sites is little more than twenty years old. The first explicit archaeological study of a site occupied by black Americans in the southern United States was Charles Fairbanks's 1968 report on excavations at the Kingsley slave cabins in Duval County, Florida.[1]

Thus, practically all of the archaeological study of black Americans has taken place in the last decade, and there has been no great burst of activity. In 1980 a volume entitled *Archaeological Perspectives on Ethnicity in America: Afro-American and Asian-American Culture History* was the first major publication to treat the archaeological investigation of black Americans.[2] The South, however, is not well represented in this work. Of the seven articles on Afro-American cultural history, only two treat topics concerning the archaeology of blacks in the South.[3] The other articles represent investigations of nineteenth- and twentieth-century Afro-American sites in the northeastern United States.

Included in the section on Afro-American cultural history in Schuyler's volume is an annotated bibliography on the archaeology of black American culture.[4] In this bibliography are twenty-two references to archaeological studies of black American culture in the South. The earliest of these was a preliminary report in 1968 on the Kingsley slave cabins.[5] Of these twenty-two, nine are formal, scholarly publications; the others are newsletter items or unpublished manuscripts. Of the nine publications only six treat black Americans as a major aspect of the work. From this accounting we see that there have been less than ten articles published on the archaeology of black Americans in the South.

Most of these articles describe, discuss, and analyze materials excavated from slave cabins identified as such from historical records. Archaeologists conducting this work have sought information on architecture and domestic refuse in an effort to reconstruct better the material components of the lifeways of Afro-Americans. Articles resulting from one report illustrated that the status differences between slave, overseer, and planter are recognizable in the archaeological record.[6] In another, pottery long thought to have been made by Indians and traded for use by slaves has been found to be very abundant in the southern colonies.[7] This pottery, it is now believed, was probably made by slaves and perhaps represents the most consistent existing record of the expression of Afro-Americans from the antebellum period.

To this point, historical archaeology and the new study of black Americans through archaeology have served primarily to furnish illustrations for the narrative written by historians. Archaeologists have been able to show exactly where slaves lived as well as examples of the dishes they used, the tools they made, and bones from the food they ate. When one is able to stand on the very spot or hold the very dish that was used by a person who lived the past of black Americans, one communes with that person in a special way. Archaeology, however, can provide more than this. The house foundations, dishes, tools, and bones were deposited in the ground directly from the hands of black Americans, and this is an exciting prospect. Throughout North Carolina and the rest of the South a record of the activity of past black Americans exists that has not passed through the filter of a white man's pen. Here is a record of black history that came directly from the hands of the people who lived it. The challenge is to learn to read it. With the aid of the oral and written historical record, archaeology can provide a totally new way of knowing about the past of black Americans.

History and Archaeology

In the relatively recent past, "history," our view of the past, has been derived solely from the scholarly interpretation of such artifacts as documents, diaries, newspapers, and books that compose the written record. Prior to the development in America and other parts of the world of the primacy of the written word in interpreting history (a technique borrowed from the elite of past generations), most people learned about the past from living informants. Historical information was once passed on primarily by word of mouth. Only within the past millenium, and especially within the last century, has the efficiency of the written word come to dominate the general view of history. The archaeological analysis of objects and other remains is a third way of learning about the past.

The usual interpretation of the history of black Americans, as derived from the written record, has been biased. It has not given a truthful and comprehensive view of the past. Furthermore, the documentary information upon which we have based our most common understandings of Afro-Americans is a biased record, written by a small portion of the population that was primarily white, male, and economically affluent. In contrast, the archaeological record, those things left in the ground from past activities, is a record of the masses. It is, simply, the most democratic record of the past that exists.

Sensitive historians have done an admirable job of reinterpreting the written records of the past so that they more faithfully represent the story of black Americans as well as those of other poor people including American Indians and a large portion of the white population. Yet even these historians are constrained by the limitations of a surviving written record that deals principally with the interests of the economically powerful. Different factors led to the creation of the archaeological record. It is the record of the poor as well as the rich, the family as well as the marketplace. When one's concern is with the whole range of past activities, the archaeological record is more general and more comprehensive than the written record.

To mitigate the problem of bias in the written record, historians have turned to oral history. Through oral history they have sought, and produced, a better story of the past. But oral history has its drawbacks. It is biased by the selectivity and limitations of human memory, and it is severely limited in span of time. Archaeological techniques do not rely on human memory. Furthermore, one of the greatest strengths of archaeological analysis ameliorates the greatest weakness of oral history: through archaeological study we can span great lengths of time.

Archaeological techniques are used to study a record that was unknowingly produced by the majority of the people as a by-product of everyday activities. Adding archaeology to the study of the Afro-American past offers the opportunity to examine an abundant record that was not produced *about* black Americans but was created *by* them.

The Abundance of the Archaeological Record

To most people the amount of material in the archaeological record is a surprise. A popular conception exists that only occasionally do archaeologists find artifacts surviving from the past. In fact, archaeological investigations often produce, from only a few months of excavation, tens of thousands of artifacts ranging from postholes and house foundations to needles, buttons, and dishes. In addition to the artifacts themselves, maps and notes describing the relationships of the artifacts provide information critical to the interpretation of the remains.

As an example, the excavation of one site apparently occupied by slaves produced evidence of a house constructed on a post foundation and five pits that were apparently dug for clay (perhaps for making pottery or daub walls) and subsequently filled with refuse.[8] Unfortunately, the floor and yard of this house had been churned up by plowing and had been scraped off by a bulldozer prior to the beginning of the excavation, so perhaps as many artifacts were lost as were recovered. Nevertheless, from the features of the site that were beneath the plow, the archaeologists recovered more than three thousand historic artifacts from the slave-period occupation. This 1978 excavation represented the first excavation of an Afro-American house site in South Carolina, a state where the majority of people over most of the history of the colony and the state has been Afro-American.[9]

The abundance of artifacts that finds its way into the ground around activity areas may be illustrated by examples of modern deposition of artifacts. Outside of Hamilton College on the campus of the University of South Carolina at a college bus stop, an area between the sidewalk and the street was examined for artifacts. Glancing at this small plot while walking along the sidewalk, no one would think that it looks especially messy. One must look closely to see that there are small, seemingly insignificant artifacts lying on the ground, such as cigarette butts, pop tops, and other items dropped by people as they waited for the bus, walked along the sidewalk, or crossed the street. There is a trash basket near the bus stop, and most people deposit their trash in that basket. When all of the artifacts were collected from that small plot of ground, however, an amazing quantity and variety of artifacts had been found. Many pieces of imported granite gravel and hundreds of small brick fragments were left on the ground. But the collection of cigarette butts, pop tops, pencil stubs, paper clips, chewing gum, pieces of tin foil, and so forth (less than 25 percent of the easily visible artifacts), amounted to 220 pieces (see Table 2-1), including two pieces of a Moon Traveler bottle rocket from Hunan, China.

Another collection was made on the grounds of the South Carolina statehouse. Around one of the park benches 78 artifacts were picked up in ten minutes in an area that is policed daily by the groundkeepers (see Table 2-2). A third ten-minute collection of 177 artifacts was made at a busy downtown bus stop where working people catch the bus (see Table 2-3). If there had been a more diligent search, if the top few inches of soil from these areas had been excavated and sifted, thousands of artifacts made, used, and deposited as by-products of human activity would doubtless have been recovered. From such collections an archaeological record grows every day. People leave an imprint of their activities that is hardly noticed. The same is even more true of the past.

Today people live a life-style in which most of their activities take place indoors. They sweep up the debris of their activities and ship it to a general dump. What is more, they are continuously cautioned not to litter. In the past people conducted more activities outside. In a yard or on a dirt floor small artifacts find their way into the ground and leave a record that linoleum floors and concrete patios cannot foster. The archaeological record of black Americans is so massive that if every scrap of it were collected, it would probably fill every library building in the United States from basement to attic and still require more storage space.

Reading the Archaeological Record

The task of reading the archaeological record involves careful examination of the entire group of artifacts, including their form, the frequency of their occurrence, and their distribution in space. Recently, Stanley South has demonstrated that in additon to the dramatic exposure of house foundations and rare specimens for museum display, thorough study of archaeological pattern analysis of historic sites can offer a powerful means for studying past activity.[10] Conducting such an analysis, Patrick Garrow has recently offered a "Carolina Slave Pattern" that he believes will

Table 2-1. *College Bus Stop Collection*

Artifact Category	Description	Count
Glass	Within this category were pieces of flat window glass, beer and soda bottle glass, as well as fragments of other types of glass artifacts.	65
Cigarette butts	Cigarette butts with and without filters were found. The filters included some with brown filter paper and some with white filter paper. Some of the butts were marked with yellow street-marking paint.	87
Pull tabs	Three distinctive types of pull tabs and fragments of tabs were found.	18
Plastic	Three types of plastic were recovered, one of which had a square hole, a round hole, the embossed numeral 2 and letter A.	9
Ceramics	Four types of late-nineteenth-century or twentieth-century ceramics were recovered.	6
Metal	Five types of metal including a tire weight, a paper clip, a nail, and a Michelob beer bottle cap were collected.	5
Chewing gum	Three green, two white, and one pink pieces of chewing gum were collected.	6
Miscellaneous	Numerous items were found in counts of only one or two including a band-aid; a rubber band; a pencil and pencil fragments; two spent Moon Traveler bottle rockets made in Hunan, China; used paper matches; fragments of food; a crayon; a drug prescription label; a fragment of paper with a drugstore name on it; as well as many other items.	24
Total artifacts		220

Table 2-2. *Capitol Park Bench Collection*

Artifact Category	Description	Count
Peanut shells		27
Cigarette butts	Butts with filters and without filters were collected. Filter papers included those that were white, brown, and dark brown.	11
Paper	Most of the pieces of paper recovered from this site were from food wrappers. In addition, a torn Visa credit card receipt, a receipt for $26.40, and fragments of a personal check were collected.	18
Plastic	Most of the plastic collected from this site was from food packages.	12
Foil	Metal foil came from food packages and over-the-counter medicine packages.	5
Miscellaneous	Wooden match sticks, a pull tab, and pieces of carbon made up this category.	5
Total artifacts		78

discriminate between the homes of bondmen and other types of colonial sites.[11]

The character of these artifact patterns and how they are "read" may be clarified by a reconsideration of the "college bus stop" site, the "park bench" site, and the "Sumter Street bus stop" site (Tables 2-1, 2-2, and 2-3). Looking at the college bus stop collection, the pencil stubs, the rubber band, the paper clip, and the crayon fragment are immediately recognizable as artifacts that might be found on a school ground. The lead tire weight suggests that the site is near a street. The peanut shells are equally characteristic of park activities. The transfer tickets indicate that the Sumter Street bus stop is on the main Columbia city bus line. Thus, the basic presence and absence of artifacts of specific form are indicative of the different settings of these two types of sites.

Not only does the form of these two collections of artifacts vary, but different activities indicated, such as drinking, eating, and smoking (Table 2-4), reveal diverse patterns of behavior at the two kinds of locations. For example, compared to eating, more smoking takes place at the bus stop sites than at the park bench

Table 2-3. *Sumter Street Bus Stop Collection*

Artifact Category	Description	Count
Cigarette butts	Cigarette butts with and without filter were collected. The majority of the filters had brown rather than white filter paper.	82
Tobacco packages	This category included cigarette packages, cigar wrappers, and cigarette tax stamps.	8
Match books	Printed information on these match books included "Food Town" and "The Army Education Center, Ft. Jackson, S.C."	4
Plastic	Plastic artifacts from this site were primarily from food packages. Four plastic drinking straws were collected, and one piece of a nonfood plastic package was labeled "Intermagnetics 8-Track Cartridge" with a Kress price tag for $2.00.	23
Foil	These pieces of foil came primarily from food packages.	9
Paper	Paper artifacts included food wrappers, paper towels, price tags, a slip of paper with an address, a fragment of paper with an address, a fragment of a welfare form, a card with a religious statement, a bus transfer, a Jovan Musk Oil box, and a Whoo Pee Cushion label.	36
Food	Food included chicken bones and a partially eaten orange.	3
Styrofoam	These artifacts included cups and other fragments of styrofoam.	8
Miscellaneous	Artifacts with counts of only one or two included wooden stirring sticks, a pull tab, and a screw-type soda cap.	4
Total artifacts		177

site. People smoke and eat in both places, but they are likely to smoke more at a bus stop and eat more at a park bench. Similarly, the evidence suggests more drinking at the bus stop than eating, whereas at the park bench there is more evidence of eating than drinking. Again, this is to be expected. It is much more common

Table 2-4. *Artifacts by Activity Groups*

	Capitol Park Bench	College Bus Stop	Sumter St. Bus Stop
Smoking	15	90	92
Eating	52	8	39
Drinking	1	77	13
Transportation	0	5	3
Business	2	1	5
Other	8	39	25
Total	78	220	177

to see people walking along or waiting for a bus with a soda can in their hand than to see them trying to eat their lunch while performing such transient activities. In examining these data different artifact patterns disclose varied types of behavior. The beginnings of a pattern emerge.

By collecting artifacts from other park bench locations and other bus stop locations the range of form and frequency of artifacts from these two different types of sites could be assessed. Subsequently, presented with a group of artifacts, the collection might be said to fit the "park bench pattern," the "college bus stop pattern," or the "city bus stop pattern." Of course this could be refined. Differences might exist in the patterns of artifacts left at a bus stop by students of a Bible college and those of a state university. The debris around a park bench next to a city playground would probably differ recognizably from one on the statehouse grounds. The distinctions would depend primarily upon the care and faithfulness with which the collections were made and the skill involved in recognizing statistically significant differences.

In modern daily life there is little need to read the material record for such information. The park bench or the bus stop sign are easily observed. Further back in time, however, such analyses take on a special importance, especially with regard to the history of black Americans. Slaves built most of the colonial South. Towns such as Charleston and Wilmington were built by slave craftsmen and slave laborers. These cities stand as monuments (although usually unrecognized) to their handiwork. On the other hand, the homes of slaves, especially on plantations, were most often post, log, or frame structures, of which little remains visible today. Excavations of these sites usually reveal the foundations. These are usually simple—a line of posts or a few piles of rocks. However, South's pattern analysis indicates that by carefully recovering all of the small artifacts from one of these sites, by plotting their location, and by examining their form and frequency of occurrence, patterns distinctive to slave home sites will emerge. These sites will be different from the sites of other people in other social and economic situations.

This type of analysis need not be limited to making gross distinctions about one site's having been occupied by slaves while another was occupied by free whites. The variable use of material things means that different people, different groups of people, and different kinds of activity involve statistically distinguishable groups of artifacts. And, when these activities result in even the smallest artifacts being deposited in the archaeological record, they leave evidence that can conceivably be found and connected to that person, group, or activity. There is the potential to distinguish between houses that were occupied by a few people and those occupied by very large families. Smokehouses, cane mills, stock barns, and rice houses can be identified. The places where people cooked, where they butchered animals, where they sat under a tree and talked can be discovered. The possibilities seem endless.

The Development of a Methodology

It is obvious that history and archaeology deal with different kinds of information. Because of this difference, there are some questions that can be dealt with only through written or oral sources. For example, archaeology will never be able to impart how it felt to be a slave. Oral history can provide this information. Written history furnishes details of the social, economic, and political pressures that stimulated slave revolts. Archaeology could provide information about these topics, but it would be quite general.

On the other hand, archaeology can provide information on the exact settlement pattern of slaves on southern plantations. Archaeology, rather than the records of owners or the casual and often biased comments of travelers, can provide concrete information on the foods that slaves ate. What is more, archaeology can produce this kind of information for many more locations than historical records can. From the examination of slave skeletons archaeology can yield information about slave nutrition and disease that is not available in any historical records. In these ways archaeology can provide a special added dimension to the study of the history of black Americans. But to do so will require the assistance of historians in developing these tools.

Historians can help tie the artifactual record to human groups and behavior. For example, working together with historians, archaeologists need to find examples of the best-documented and best-preserved sites of black Americans from all time periods. Archaeologists need historical information about the location of slave quarters, barns, field quarters, and so forth. Particularly valuable are examples of houses that burned at known dates or houses that were occupied by families of known size. Archaeologists need to excavate slave communities where masters kept careful records of the food that they were supplying. Then, to advance the archaeological aspect of this methodological development, they can choose from these well-documented locations the ones best preserved. By excavating these sites and developing a body of patterned archaeological information, an analogue to known behavior can be constructed. With this body of information archaeologists will be able to conduct surveys and identify sites that were not reported or were poorly represented in the written and oral evidence. Consequently, archaeology will be able to answer many questions beyond the limitations of written or oral history.

Conclusion

Unfortunately, there are no detailed examples of the power of using analyses that combine the best of archaeology and history to provide extraordinary elucidations of the story of black Americans. This is not because attempts have been made and failed, however. It is because such attempts have only recently begun. Archaeologists are just beginning to recognize the means for capitalizing on the material record of the past, just beginning to work with historians to develop the methodology. The development of the methodology is going to be difficult. It is going to cost a lot of money. Yet developing archaeology and history into a rigorous means of studying the past will expand beyond our imaginations our opportunity to know about the past of black Americans.

NOTES

1. Charles H. Fairbanks, "The Kingsley Slave Cabins in Duval County, Florida, 1968," *The Conference on Historic Sites Archaeology Papers*, vol. 7 (n.p., 1972), pp. 62–93.

2. Robert L. Schuyler, ed., *Archaeological Perspectives on Ethnicity in America: Afro-American and Asian-American Culture History* (New York: Baywood Publishing Company, 1980).

3. John Solomon Otto, "Race and Class on Antebellum Plantations," ibid., pp. 3–13; Leland G. Ferguson, "Looking for the 'Afro' in Colono-Indian Pottery," ibid., pp. 14–28.

4. Geoffrey M. Gyrisco and Bert Salwen, comps., "Archaeology of Black American Culture: An Annotated Bibliography," ibid., pp. 76–85.

5. Charles H. Fairbanks, "The Kingsley Slave Cabins in Duval County, Florida," paper delivered at the Conference on Historic Sites Archaeology, 1968.

6. John Solomon Otto, "Status Differences and the Archaeological Record: A Comparison of Planter, Overseer, and Slave Sites from Cannon's Point Plantation, 1794–1861, St. Simon's Island, Georgia," Ph.D. diss., University of Florida, 1975. From this research Otto has published two essays: "Race and Class on Antebellum Plantations," cited above, and "Artifacts and Status Differences: A Comparison of Ceramics from Planter, Overseer, and Slave Sites on an Antebellum Plantation," in Stanley South, ed., *Research Strategies in Historical Archaeology* (New York: Academic Press, 1977), pp. 91–118.

7. Ferguson, "Colono-Indian Pottery."

8. Lesley M. Drucker and Ronald W. Anthony, *The Spiers Landing*

Site: Archaeological Investigations in Berkeley County, South Carolina (Atlanta: U.S. Department of the Interior, 1979), p. 123.

9. Julian J. Petty, *The Growth and Distribution of Population in South Carolina* (Columbia, S.C.: State Council for Defense, 1943); Peter H. Wood, *Black Majority: Negroes in Colonial South Carolina from 1670 through the Stono Rebellion* (New York: Norton, 1974), p. 152.

10. Stanley South, *Method and Theory in Historical Archaeology* (New York: Academic Press, 1977).

11. Patrick H. Garrow, "Investigations of Yaughan and Curriboo Plantations," a paper delivered at the Southeastern Archaeological Conference, 1980, at New Orleans, Louisiana.

3. A Demographic Analysis of Colonial North Carolina with Special Emphasis upon the Slave and Black Populations

Marvin L. Michael Kay and Lorin Lee Cary

While concentrating upon some of the demographic characteristics of the slave population in North Carolina during the years 1748 to 1772, this essay will also deal with pertinent demographic characteristics of free blacks, servants, and whites. Immigration, growth, and geographical population patterns will be analyzed for both black and white North Carolinians, but population density, the comparative concentration of workers on large units of production, sex ratios, and sex imbalance ratios (calculated for each plantation) will be analyzed only for blacks. The examination of sex ratios for blacks will lead to a discussion of the causal connection between the lessening sex disparity among slaves in the colony and the increasing numerical importance of native-born slaves as compared with those born in Africa. The number and proportion of blacks who were free will also be assessed, along with the disproportionate tendency of free blacks to become servants. Although slaves gradually replaced servants as colonial North Carolina's most numerous unfree laborers, both types of labor continued to make up a significant portion of the colony's work force until the Revolution. Numbers of servants will be estimated and an attempt made to determine the sexual and racial composition of this important segment of colonial North Carolina's population, one long neglected by almost all students interested in the history of the province.[1] Finally, some attention will be paid to the illegal enslavement of free blacks and black servants.

North Carolina's original slave population, probably numbering around 1,000 during the first decade of the eighteenth century, came, as did their masters, from Virginia.[2] At this time the colony's few slaves remained concentrated in the Albemarle Sound region in the northeastern coastal portion of North Carolina, bordering or close to Virginia. From the last decade of the seventeenth century, however, immigrants from Virginia, some with slaves, not only continued to settle the Albemarle but also moved south to the area around the Tar, Neuse, and Trent rivers, all of which emptied into Pamlico Sound. These last settlers were joined by immigrants coming directly from France, Switzerland, and the Palatinate. The population of the Neuse-Pamlico region consequently grew gradually, along with that of the Albemarle area, during the first decades of the eighteenth century. By the 1720s the Cape Fear region was also being settled, as whites with their slaves, mostly from South Carolina, moved into the southeastern portion of North Carolina.[3] In 1732, in what is perhaps the most reliable early population estimate, Governor George Burrington placed the provincial population at about 30,000 whites and 6,000 blacks.[4]

In the ensuing years areas west of the Outer Coastal Plain began to be settled. From the 1730s onward, a strong outflow of whites streamed westward from the Albemarle region, the Neuse-Pamlico region, and to a limited degree the Lower Cape Fear region to help settle four areas to the westward: the Upper Cape Fear region, the Central and Northern Inner Plain–Piedmont regions, and the Western region (see Tables 3-1, 3-2, and 3-3). Of probably greater numerical significance in the settling of the latter two areas from the 1750s on, however, were migrants from Virginia and other colonies to the northward, especially Maryland and Pennsylvania. Unlike earlier migrants, these newcomers from the provinces to the north very likely were not predominantly of English stock. Waves of Scotch-Irish and German migrants took up land in Orange, Anson, Rowan, and Mecklenburg counties and probably dominated the latter two most westerly counties. Meanwhile, primarily in the 1760s and 1770s, Highland Scots came directly from Scotland to help populate the Upper Cape Fear

River counties of Bladen and Cumberland and to settle as far west as Anson County.[5]

Both natural increase and the influx of immigrants explain why North Carolina's white population more than doubled to about 65,000 between 1730 and 1755, an annual growth rate of about 3 percent. The white population—with the increased inflow of migrants from the north and, though less significant, directly from Europe—grew even more rapidly in the next twelve years. By 1767 whites numbered about 124,000, a net gain of 89 percent since 1755, and about a 5.1 percent annual rate of growth (see Tables 3-1, 3-2, and 3-3).

The number of blacks expanded even more dramatically during these years. From about 1,000 in 1705 the black population grew rapidly to roughly 6,000 in 1730, a yearly rate of growth of 5.7 percent. Although the rate of increase dropped to a still high 4.1 percent during the next twenty-five years, this more than tripled the black population to about 19,000 by 1755. Over the next twelve years North Carolina's black population experienced its most rapid and significant increase—more than doubling to nearly 41,000 by 1767, a 6.2 percent yearly growth rate (see Tables 3-1, 3-2, and 3-3).

Scholars have uniformly stressed both immigration and natural increase to explain the rapid growth of North Carolina's white population. Despite even higher growth rates for the black population, however, some scholars have erroneously concluded that this rapid expansion between 1730 and 1767 may be explained almost entirely by natural increase. To support this contention they have noted that the scattered extant records of entries of slaves through North Carolina's seaports indicate that "even in the busiest years" relatively few slaves, perhaps no more than one or two hundred per year, entered North Carolina directly from Africa or from the West Indies prior to the Revolution.[6]

Despite such evidence the growth rate of blacks in North Carolina during these years must challenge the conclusion that it could be explained almost solely by natural increase. Between 1730 and 1755 the black population increased 209 percent (from 6,000 to 18,532), a 4.1 percent yearly growth rate, and from 1755 to 1767

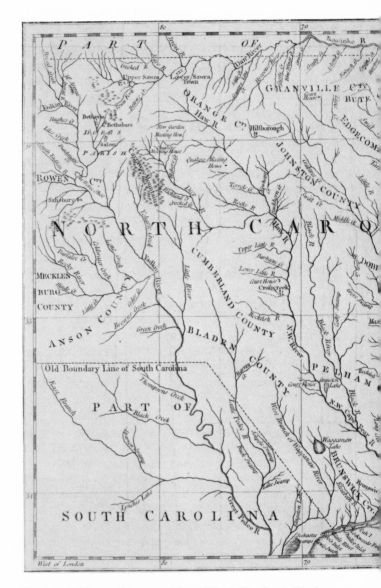

Fig. 3-1. "A New and Accurate Map of North Carolina in North America" first appeared in 1779 in the *Universal Magazine*, published

by J. Hinton in London. From Map Collection, North Carolina Division
of Archives and History, Raleigh.

Table 3-1. *Population Statistics for North Carolina's Regions and Counties for the Years 1755 and 1767*

Regions and Counties	1755			1767		
	Totals[1]	Whites	Blacks	Totals	Whites	Blacks
Albemarle	22,108[30]	(16,973)	(5,135)	28,517	(18,343)	(10,174)
Sound Region:	13,393[31]	10,561	2,832	21,141	13,379	7,762
Currituck[2]	2,227	1,943	284	2,543[32]	(1,980)	(563)
Pasquotank[3]	3,000	2,308	692	4,179[33]	3,034	1,145
Perquimans[4]	3,857	(2,809)	(1,048)	4,083[34]	2,161	1,922
Chowan[5]	4,858	(3,603)	(1,255)	4,571[35]	2,526	2,045
Hertford[6]	—	—	—	4,833[36]	(2,984)	(1,849)
Bertie[7]	5,577	4,354	1,223	5,136[37]	3,223	1,913
Tyrrell[8]	2,589	1,956	633	3,172[38]	2,435	737
Neuse-Pamlico	15,176	(11,302)	(3,874)	23,970	17,274	6,696
Region:	13,769	10,185	3,584			
Hyde[9]	1,412	1,132	280	2,341[39]	1,808	533
Beaufort-Pitt[10]	4,233	3,161	1,072	6,750[40]	4,953	1,797
Craven[11]	5,820	4,055	1,765	8,523[41]	5,650	2,873
Carteret[12]	1,407	(1,117)	(290)	2,475[42]	1,927	548
Onslow[13]	2,304	1,837	467	3,881[43]	2,936	945
Lower Cape Fear Region:	4,308	1,624	2,684	7,942[44]	2,997	4,945
New Hanover[14]	4,308	1,624	2,684	4,973[45]	2,079	2,894
Brunswick[15]	—	—	—	2,969[46]	918	2,051
Upper Cape Fear Region:	2,040	1,386	654	4,596	3,243	1,353
Bladen[16]	2,040	1,386	654	4,596[47]	3,243	1,353
Central Inner Plain–Piedmont Region:	9,424	8,216	1,208	21,872	17,909	3,963

Table 3-1. *(continued)*

Regions and Counties	1755			1767		
	Totals[1]	Whites	Blacks	Totals	Whites	Blacks
Dobbs[17]	—	—	—	6,533[48]	5,199	1,334
Johnston[18]	5,842	5,092	750	5,701[49]	4,629	1,072
Duplin[19]	2,204	1,886	318	5,217[50]	4,391	826
Cumberland[20]	1,378	1,238	140	4,421[51]	3,690	731
Northern Inner Plain–Piedmont Region:	18,511	13,985	4,526	36,790 13,006	(26,352) 9,516	(10,438) 3,490
Northampton[21]	5,274	3,698	1,576	7,978[52]	(5,362)	(2,616)
Halifax[22]	—	—	—	8,755[53]	(6,210)	(2,545)
Edgecombe[23]	8,925	6,863	2,062	7,051[54]	(5,264)	(1,787)
Bute[24]	—	—	—	7,104[55]	5,326	1,778
Granville[25]	4,312	3,424	888	5,902[56]	4,190	1,712
Western Region:	12,378	11,927	451	40,749 19,208	(37,677) 17,503	(3,072) 1,705
Orange[26]	4,266	4,030	236	16,027[57]	14,649	1,378
Rowan[27]	4,678	4,576	102	13,516[58]	(12,797)	(719)
Anson[28]	3,434	3,321	113	3,181[59]	2,854	327
Mecklenburg[29]	—	—	—	8,025[60]	(7,377)	(648)

1. Taxable totals may be found in the various sources listed below. White and black taxable totals were converted into population totals by using multipliers, respectively, of 4.1 and 1.89. The varying size of the multipliers reflects the proportion of each population legally defined as taxables and the age distribution within each of the two populations. Since all blacks, male and female, who were twelve and over were taxables, but only white males sixteen and over were taxables, it is understandable why a much greater proportion of the black population appeared on the tax lists. The smaller black multiplier primarily reflects this fact.

Since very few data exist that list the black and white populations according to age, the sample used to calculate the age distribution of blacks and whites, a Pitt County 1775 tax list, was necessarily small and insufficiently representative.

Nonetheless, Pitt County in 1775 is not an outlandish choice since its comparatively immature state is significantly offset by the late date of the sample. Whatever the case, we believe it is the best extant sample.

Extrapolations had to be made when white and black population totals were lacking. These will be described below in appropriate notes. A word, however, is in order to describe the method used to convert, when necessary, taxable totals (blacks together with whites) into population totals. This task is complicated by the fact that the comparative size of the two populations, black and white, helps to define the size of the multiplier in addition to the variables noted above. This necessitated that we develop multipliers for each region for ca. 1755 and ca. 1767. The methods used will be described below, but the calculated regional multipliers are: Albemarle–3.28, 2.86; Neuse-Pamlico–3.14, 3.09; Lower Cape Fear–2.37, 2.36; Upper Cape Fear–2.98, 3.04; Central Inner Plain–Piedmont–3.56, 3.36; Northern Inner Plain–Piedmont–3.18, 3.12; West–3.93, 3.71.

The 1775 Pitt County tax list from which the multipliers for white and black taxables were obtained may be found in Tax Lists, 1720–1839, Secretary of State Papers, North Carolina State Archives.

2. Saunders, ed., *Colonial Records*, 5:575.

3. Ibid.

4. Ibid., for taxable total—1,176. The multiplier 3.28 was used to obtain the total population, 3,857. The percentage of Perquimans County's population that was black in 1755 was calculated by multiplying the percentage of the Albemarle Sound region's population that was black in 1755 by the percentage of Perquimans County's population that was black in 1767 and dividing the result by the percentage of the region's population that was black in 1767. Black and white population totals for 1755 were, in turn, calculated for the county from the percentage obtained above.

5. See Saunders, ed., *Colonial Records*, 5:575, for taxable total—1,481. See note 4 for procedures used to obtain white and black population totals. The multiplier 3.28 was used to convert the taxable total to total population, 4,858.

6. Hertford County was formed from Chowan, Bertie, and Northampton counties in 1759.

7. We used the white-black breakdown for 1751 and the taxable total for 1754 to calculate Bertie figures for 1755. For 1751 figures see Colonial Court Records, Taxes and Accounts, 1679–1754, North Carolina State Archives. For 1754 totals see Saunders, ed., *Colonial Records*, 5:320.

8. Saunders, ed., *Colonial Records*, 5:575.

9. Lists of Taxables, Militia and Magistrates, 1754–70, and undated, in Governors Office Papers, North Carolina State Archives.

10. Saunders, ed., *Colonial Records*, 5:575. Pitt was formed from Beaufort County in 1760.

11. Ibid.

12. The estimated taxable total equals the mean for the years 1754 and 1756: 448. See Broadside, "Table of Taxables in the Province of North Carolina from 1748 . . . to 1770," Massachusetts Historical Society, as quoted in Evarts S.

Greene and Virginia D. Harrington, *American Population before the Federal Census of 1790* (New York: Columbia University Press, 1932), p. 162. See note 4 for general procedures used to calculate the white and black population totals. The multiplier to obtain the population total from the taxable total in the Neuse-Pamlico region is 3.14.

13. Saunders, ed., *Colonial Records*, 5:575.

14. See Tax Lists, Treasurers and Comptrollers Papers, North Carolina State Archives.

15. Brunswick County was formed from New Hanover and Bladen counties in 1764.

16. Lists of Taxables, Militia and Magistrates, 1754–70, and undated, in Governors Office Papers, North Carolina State Archives.

17. Dobbs County was formed from Johnston County in 1758.

18. Lists of Taxables, Militia and Magistrates, 1754–70, and undated, in Governors Office Papers, North Carolina State Archives.

19. Saunders, ed., *Colonial Records*, 5:575.

20. Lists of Taxables, Militia and Magistrates, 1754–70, and undated, in Governors Office Papers, North Carolina State Archives.

21. Saunders, ed., *Colonial Records*, 5:575.

22. Halifax County was formed from Edgecombe County in 1759.

23. Lists of Taxables, Militia and Magistrates, 1754–70, and undated, in Governors Office Papers, North Carolina State Archives.

24. Bute County was formed from Granville County in 1764.

25. Lists of Taxables, Militia and Magistrates, 1754–70, and undated, in Governors Office Papers, North Carolina State Archives.

26. Tax Lists, Treasurers and Comptrollers Papers, North Carolina State Archives.

27. Saunders, ed., *Colonial Records*, 5:575.

28. Ibid.

29. Mecklenburg County was formed from Anson County in 1762.

30. Totals for all existing counties in the region.

31. Totals for all existing counties in region except for those whose estimates are in parentheses. The same pattern obtains for each region that has two totals.

32. Currituck's total taxables were obtained from Saunders, ed., *Colonial Records*, 7:539. The taxable total, 889, was multiplied by 2.86 to estimate the county's total population in 1767—2,543. The percentage of Currituck County's population that was black was calculated by multiplying the percentage of the Albemarle Sound's population that was black in 1767 by the percentage of Currituck County's population that was black in 1755 and dividing the result by the percentage of the region that was black in 1755. Black and white population totals for 1767 were, in turn, calculated for the county from the percentage obtained above.

33. The listing of taxables is incomplete for Pasquotank County in 1767. We therefore used the figures for 1766. See Saunders, ed., *Colonial Records*, 7:288–89.

34. Saunders, ed., *Colonial Records*, 7:288–89. The figures for Perquimans County are for 1766.

35. Saunders, ed., *Colonial Records*, 7:288–89. The figures for Chowan County are for 1766.

36. Hertford County's taxable total, 1,690, was obtained from Saunders, ed., *Colonial Records*, 7:539. Since Hertford did not exist in 1755, a procedure different from that used for Currituck had to be devised to estimate Hertford's white and black populations for 1767. This was roughly achieved by taking the average distribution in the three counties from which Hertford was formed: Bertie, Chowan, and Northampton. The multiplier used to convert Hertford's taxable total to total population was 2.86.

37. The listing of taxables for Bertie County is incomplete for 1767. We therefore extrapolated from lists for the years 1766 and 1768 to arrive at the 1767 population figures. That is, we added one-half the population differences between the two years to the totals for 1766 to calculate the 1767 population. See List of Taxables, Bertie County, 1765–71, North Carolina State Archives.

38. Saunders, ed., *Colonial Records*, 7:539.

39. Ibid.

40. See ibid. for Beaufort County. We, however, used 1766 totals for Pitt County. See Saunders, ed., *Colonial Records*, 7:288–89.

41. Saunders, ed., *Colonial Records*, 7:539.

42. Ibid.

43. Ibid.

44. The increases for the Lower Cape Fear are exaggerated, while those for the Upper Cape Fear are underestimated. This is so because a portion of Bladen County was incorporated into Brunswick County when it was formed in 1764. The distortions cannot be corrected.

45. New Hanover County's totals are for 1766. See Saunders, *Colonial Records*, 7:288–89.

46. Ibid., p. 539.

47. Ibid.

48. Ibid.

49. Ibid.

50. Ibid.

51. We used records for 1766 for Cumberland County because they are more complete than those for 1767. See Saunders, ed., *Colonial Records*, 7:288–89.

52. See Saunders, ed., *Colonial Records*, 7:539, for taxable totals. Northampton County's multiplier to obtain population totals is 3.12. See note 32 for procedures to get 1767 population breakdown.

53. We averaged the percentages of blacks that lived in Northampton and Edgecombe counties in 1767 to obtain the percentage of blacks who lived in Halifax County. We then used this percentage to calculate the county's white and black population in 1767. The total number of taxables was found in Saunders, ed., *Colonial Records*, 7:539. Multiplier is 3.12.

the number rose even more remarkably: 111 percent (from 18,532 to 40,641), more than a 6 percent yearly growth rate (see Tables 3-2 and 3-3). Allan Kulikoff, studying the black populations of Virginia and Maryland, has recently concluded that by "mid-eighteenth century, one ought to expect the adult population to increase naturally by about 2.5 percent a year without further immigration from Africa. Any growth rate under 2.5 percent would indicate outmigration; any figure greatly above 2.5 percent would suggest immigration of Creoles or immigrants."[7]

There appears to be little doubt, therefore, that the large increase in the number of slaves in North Carolina during the second third of the eighteenth century can be explained in part by immigration to the colony. Indeed, probably more than half the increase in black population for the years 1755 to 1767 can be so explained.

How was this the case despite the contradictory tale told by North Carolina's official immigration figures for blacks? First, the scanty evidence that appears in extant newspapers about imported slaves hints at lax record-keeping practices by officials at North Carolina ports of entry. During a single two-month period in the fall of 1764 newspaper advertisements disclosed that at least fifty slaves were imported, many of them from Barbados, which suggests the continuance of a practice observed by John Brickell in the 1730s.[8] This total is higher than figures obtained from extant official import records.

But lax record keeping at North Carolina's ports does not alone

54. See Saunders, ed., *Colonial Records*, 7:539, for taxable total. See note 32 for procedures. Multiplier is 3.12.

55. Saunders, ed., *Colonial Records*, 7:539.

56. Ibid.

57. Ibid.

58. Ibid., for taxable total. Multiplier is 3.71. See note 32 for procedures.

59. Saunders, ed., *Colonial Records*, 7:539.

60. Mecklenburg County's white and black totals for 1767 were calculated by averaging the percentage of blacks that lived in the other three western counties. The resulting percentage was then used for Mecklenburg County. See Saunders, ed., *Colonial Records*, 7:539, for taxable total. Multiplier is 3.71.

Table 3-2. *Population Statistics for North Carolina and Its Regions*

Ca. 1755

Regions and Province	White Population Black Population Total Population	Percentage of Province's Population in Region	Percentage of Province's White Population in Region	Percentage of Province's Black Population in Region	Percentage of Blacks within Each Region and within the Province
Albemarle Sound Region	16,973 5,135 22,108	26.34	25.95	27.71	23.23
Neuse-Pamlico Region	11,302 3,874 15,176	18.08	17.28	20.90	25.53
Lower Cape Fear Region	1,624 2,684 4,308	5.13	2.48	14.48	62.30
Upper Cape Fear Region	1,386 654 2,040	2.43	2.12	3.53	32.06
Central Inner Plain–Piedmont Region	8,216 1,208 9,424	11.23	12.56	6.52	12.82
Northern Inner Plain–Piedmont Region	13,985 4,526 18,511	22.05	21.38	24.42	24.45
Western Region	11,927 451 12,378	14.75	18.23	2.43	3.64
North Carolina	65,413 18,532 83,945	100.00	100.00	100.00	22.08

Ca. 1767

White Population Black Population Total Population	Percentage of Province's Population in Region	Percentage of Province's White Popula- tion in Region	Percentage of Province's Black Popula- tion in Region	Percentage of Blacks within Each Region and within the Province
18,343 10,174 28,517	17.34	14.82	25.03	35.68
17,274 6,696 23,970	14.58	13.95	16.48	27.93
2,997 4,945 7,942	4.83	2.42	12.17	62.26
3,243 1,353 4,596	2.80	2.62	3.33	29.44
17,909 3,963 21,872	13.30	14.47	9.75	18.12
26,352 10,438 36,790	22.37	21.29	25.68	28.37
37,677 3,072 40,749	24.78	30.43	7.56	7.54
123,795 40,641 164,436	100.00	100.00	100.00	24.72

Note: Table 3-2 was calculated directly from the raw population figures in Table 3-1.

Table 3-3. *Population Increases for Each Region and the Province, ca. 1755–ca. 1767*

Regions and Province	Total Population Increase Percentage Increase Rate of Growth Per Annum[a]	White Population Increase Percentage Increase Rate of Growth Per Annum	Black Population Increase Percentage Increase Rate of Growth Per Annum
Albemarle Sound Region	6,409 28.99 2.10	1,370 8.07 .65	5,039 98.13 5.49
Neuse-Pamlico Region	8,794 57.95 3.74	5,972 52.84 3.48	2,822 72.84 4.45
Lower Cape Fear Region[b]	3,634 84.35 4.94	1,373 84.54 4.95	2,261 84.24 4.94
Upper Cape Fear Region[b]	2,556 125.29 6.42	1,857 133.98 6.69	699 106.88 5.80
Central Inner Plain–Piedmont Region	12,448 132.09 6.63	9,693 117.98 6.18	2,755 228.06 8.88
Northern Inner Plain–Piedmont Region	18,279 98.75 5.51	12,367 88.43 5.11	5,912 130.62 6.58
Western Region	28,371 229.21 8.90	25,750 215.90 8.65	2,621 581.15 12.40
North Carolina	80,491 95.89 5.40	58,382 89.25 5.14	22,109 119.30 6.23

account for many of the undiscovered black migrants to the province. Many of the slaves, like their owners and much of the province's imports and exports, came to or went from the colony by overland routes between North Carolina and its neighbors, Virginia and South Carolina. Burdened with a treacherous coastline and lacking good harbors, North Carolinians had to depend upon their provincial neighbors for marketing services and supplies. Many slaves who first entered Charleston or ports in Virginia were eventually reexported via inland river and wagon routes to North Carolina. Governor Burrington recognized this situation, if in jaundiced fashion, when in 1730 he groused that because few slaves were imported "directly from Africa," North Carolinians had "to buy the refuse, refractory, and distempered negroes brought in from other governments."[9] Robert Higgins's study of the South Carolina slave trade further supports this finding; he notes that a majority of the 70,435 to 74,098 slaves entering that colony between 1735 and 1775 were reexported primarily to Georgia and secondarily to North Carolina.[10]

It is impossible to calculate for the years 1730 to 1772 reasonably precise estimates of the numbers of African slaves who came from Africa, the West Indies, or other mainland colonies or the numbers of Creole slaves who came from the latter two areas.

---

a. Population increases were calculated from Table 3-2.
The rate of population growth was calculated from the following approximation formula:

$$r = \frac{2(P_2 - P_1)}{n(P_1 + P_2)}$$

Where:

r is the rate of population growth per annum; P_1 is the unit of population (total, white, or black) for a political unit (the province or a particular region) for the earlier period; P_2 is the unit of population for a political unit for the later period; n is the number of years between P_1 and P_2.

The source for this formula is Henry S. Shryock and Jacob S. Siegel and Associates, *The Methods and Materials of Demography*, 2 vols. (Washington, D.C.: Bureau of the Census, 1971), 2:380.
b. See note 59, Table 3-1.

Some rough estimates for slave immigrants, both African and Creole, for twelve years of this period, however, may be gleaned from statistics already cited concerning the relative numbers of slaves who came to North Carolina by sea routes and land routes. If we assume that our limited findings in newspaper advertisements are typical for the years 1755 to 1767, an extrapolation of the 50 slaves imported within a two-month period in the fall of 1764 suggests that some 3,600 slaves came to North Carolina by sea routes during this period. Assuming further that about 2.5 percent of the growth rate during the years 1755 to 1767 is explained by natural increase among the population that lived in North Carolina, then immigration accounted for over 50 percent of the growth of the slave population during these years. Since the period experienced an absolute increase of 22,109 blacks, a yearly rate of increase of 6.23 percent, it is not unreasonable to assume that during the years 1755 to 1767 approximately 12,000 blacks migrated to North Carolina and that from 55 to 70 percent of these probably came via overland routes. Recent black immigrants to North Carolina, therefore, whatever their immediate geographical origins and whether Africans or Creoles, made up a sizable proportion of North Carolina's black population in the 1750s and 1760s (see Tables 3-2 and 3-3).

Only occasional references to the African tribal origins of North Carolina's slaves remain—usually in advertisements describing runaways. Such slaves were identified as Angolan, Ibo, Mandingo, or Coramantee. All that may be added to such flimsy evidence is the suggestion that since so many of North Carolina's imported slaves came from Virginia and South Carolina, perhaps the tribal origins of the slaves in these colonies roughly corresponded to those of the slaves who lived in North Carolina. Thus, slaves living in North Carolina's northern counties probably most resembled Virginia's slaves and those living in the southern counties likely had tribal backgrounds somewhat similar to those of South Carolina's slaves.[11]

A regional analysis of population growth in North Carolina reveals that by 1755 three of the province's seven geographical regions (the Albemarle, Neuse-Pamlico, and Northern Inner

Plain–Piedmont) had black populations that equaled about one-quarter of the regional population and that in two regions, the Upper and Lower Cape Fear, blacks equaled about one-third and two-thirds, respectively, of their region's populations. By 1767 in each of three regions—the Neuse-Pamlico, Upper Cape Fear, and the Northern Inner Plain–Piedmont—blacks totaled nearly 30 percent of the population, while in two regions, the Albemarle Sound and the Lower Cape Fear, they equaled over one-third and close to two-thirds, respectively, of their populations. In a sixth region, the Central Inner Plain–Piedmont, blacks increased from one-eighth of the region's population in 1755 to nearly one-fifth in 1767. Only in the western counties did blacks remain relatively inconsequential, despite a dramatic per annum rate of increase of 12.4 percent: slaves accounted for 3.64 percent of the region's population in 1755 and 7.54 percent in 1767. For North Carolina as a whole the percentage of blacks rose from about 22 percent of the population in 1755 to about 25 percent in 1767, or from 18,945 to 40,641 (see Table 3-2).

Black population density also increased during the years 1755 to 1767 in all regions; the number of blacks per square mile increased from .43 in 1755 to .94 in 1767. The Lower Cape Fear region had the highest black population density with 1.35 blacks per square mile in 1755 and 2.49 in 1767. The Northern Inner Plain–Piedmont region, however, closely rivaled the Lower Cape Fear by 1767 with a density figure of 2.45, as compared with 1.06 in 1755. The Albemarle Sound region fell to third position in 1767 with a density figure of 2.24 (1.13 in 1755). At the other end of the spectrum were the Central Inner Plain–Piedmont, Upper Cape Fear, and Western regions; the west had only .03 and .16 blacks per square mile in 1755 and 1767, respectively (see Table 3-4).

Despite this rapid increase in population density among blacks, the number of blacks per square mile, even where they were most densely settled, remained slight in comparison with high-density regions in other provinces. For instance, historian Russell R. Menard calculates that in four contiguous tidewater counties on Maryland's lower Western Shore, the number of blacks per square mile increased from less than one and one-half in 1704 to about

Table 3-4. *Black Population, Area, and Black Population Density of North Carolina, ca. 1755 and ca. 1767.*

Region	Black Population		Land Area (square miles)	Density of Black Population	
	1755	1767		1755	1767
Albemarle Sound Region	5,135	10,174	4,541	1.13	2.24
Neuse-Pamlico Region	3,874	6,696	5,129	.76	1.31
Lower Cape Fear Region	2,684	4,945	1,989	1.35	2.49
Upper Cape Fear Region	654	1,353	3,175	.21	.43
Central Inner Plain–Piedmont Region	1,208	3,963	7,142	.17	.55
Northern Inner Plain–Piedmont Region	4,526	10,438	4,268	1.06	2.45
Western Region	451	3,072	16,890	.03	.18
North Carolina	18,532	40,641	43,134	.43	.94
North Carolina except for Western Region	18,081	37,569	26,244	.69	1.43

Sources and Methods: We wish to thank George Stevenson of the North Carolina State Archives for computing for us the square mileage totals for each of the seven geographical regions as of 1767. We then used the same figures for 1755.

four in 1730 and to over nine by 1755.[12] Unfortunately, we do not know of other density patterns with which to compare North Carolina's figures, but we suspect that many of Virginia's tidewater counties would roughly correspond with the four counties in Maryland.

However this may be, if we compare solely North Carolina's Lower Cape Fear region (1,989 square miles), where the province's blacks were most densely settled, with the four Maryland counties (1,662 square miles), the differences are dramatic. The density figures for the Chesapeake region by 1755 were more than six times those for the Lower Cape Fear. This difference probably can be explained by the later settlement and development of North Carolina and the fact that the Lower Cape Fear's dependence upon forest industries demanded that slave workers be concentrated on relatively large units of production that were dispersed over larger

---

This is yet another example of the numerous ways in which the members of the staff of the State Archives aided us in this and other research projects. They gave their time and expertise unstintingly to us, and we shall ever be profoundly grateful.

In making his computations, Mr. Stevenson in some instances had to assign areas to particular colonial regions arbitrarily. For all practical purposes, white settlements in 1767 stopped at the foothills; therefore the Blue Ridge counties of today were not computed to calculate the 1767 square mileage totals for the Western region. The same area used for the Western region in 1767 was used for 1755 despite different frontiers. This results in an underestimation of the population density of the Western region in 1755 for the actual area settled. The population density of the Lower Cape Fear possibly is slightly exaggerated, while that of the Upper Cape Fear is slightly underestimated, because a portion of Bladen County (the southeastern corner) became part of Brunswick County in 1764 when it was formed primarily from New Hanover County. Lastly, some of the areas attributed to the Albemarle Sound and the Neuse-Pamlico regions were under water. The population density figures for these regions are consequently somewhat deflated.

Density of population was calculated by using the following formula:

$$\frac{P_1}{a_1}$$

Where P_1 is the number of persons in the county 1 of the province; a_1 is the number of square miles of land area in the same county. For the entire province, the ratio is $\frac{P}{A}$, calculated from the total figures of population and land area.

land areas than was the case in the mature tobacco-producing regions of the Chesapeake. Some other regions of North Carolina, also later settled and less economically mature than the Maryland counties, did produce tobacco, but this production shared economic place with forest production, grain, and provisions. Slaves remained even more sparsely settled in those regions than in the Lower Cape Fear region.

Nonetheless, because the number of slaves increased more rapidly than did the white population and because the slaves' percentage of the total population became higher, or, as in the Lower Cape Fear, remained very high, the percentage of blacks concentrated upon large plantations either increased or remained at a high level in each region of North Carolina during the years 1750 to 1775.[13] The concentration of slaves on plantations with ten or more slaves rose from 50.7 percent in the period 1748 to 1755 to 61.6 percent in the period 1763 to 1771. The proportion of slaves residing on production units with twenty or more slaves during the same time span increased from 19.4 percent to 28.5 percent. At the same time the number and size of extremely large slaveholdings also increased.

The concentration of slaves on large plantations was most prevalent in the Lower Cape Fear: 87.9 percent of the slaves were owned by masters with ten or more slaves in the period 1748 to 1755 and 90.2 percent in the period 1763 to 1771. Respective percentages for slaves owned by masters with twenty or more slaves were 73.7 percent for the early years and 72.9 percent for the latter period. Although the concentration of slaves on such plantations was considerably less in other regions, there was also a much greater tendency for such concentrations to increase over time outside the Lower Cape Fear. This trend occurred most noticeably among those slaves living on plantations with twenty or more slaves. The percentages of slaves living on plantations with twenty or more slaves went up from the earlier period (1748-55) to the later period (1763-71) as follows: Northern Inner Plain–Piedmont—6.7 percent to 32.2 percent; Albemarle—8.5 percent to 21.1 percent; Neuse-Pamlico—14.1 percent to 19.8 percent; and Upper Cape Fear—36.8 percent to 47.5 percent (see Table 3-5).

Given the density patterns previously discussed, a comparison

Table 3-5. *Regional and Provincial Slave Ownership–Distribution Patterns (percentages of slaves in different numerical categories)*

Regions and Province	1748–55					1763–71				
	1–4	5–9	10–19	20+	Range	1–4	5–9	10–19	20+	Range
Albemarle Sound Region	32.0	23.1	36.5	8.5	27	22.9	23.0	33.0	21.1	87
Neuse-Pamlico Region	26.2	18.5	41.2	14.1	28	25.0	22.0	33.3	19.8	91
Lower Cape Fear Region	4.9	7.3	14.2	73.7	199	5.4	4.4	17.3	72.9	242
Upper Cape Fear Region	22.1	19.9	21.3	36.8	—	16.2	14.7	21.6	47.5	93
Central Inner Plain–Piedmont Region	38.5	27.3	27.1	7.1	—	32.1	23.0	33.2	11.7	47
Northern Inner Plain–Piedmont Region	32.3	30.0	31.1	6.7	55	13.0	12.7	42.1	32.2	64
Western Region	50.4	33.8	15.8	0	11	43.4	23.7	32.9	0	17
North Carolina	27.5	22.0	31.3	19.4	199	20.8	17.7	33.1	28.5	242

Sources and Methods: Slave taxable totals were converted to slave population totals in individual households by estimating that households listing 1 to 2 slave taxables owned 1 to 4 slaves; those with 3 to 4 taxables owned 5 to 9 slaves; those with 5 to 10 taxables owned 10 to 19 slaves; and those with 11 or more taxables owned 20 or more slaves. Taxes and Accounts, 1679–1754, Colonial Court Records; Lists of Taxables, 1765–71, Bertie County Records; Lists of Taxables, 1771, Bute County Records; Lists of Taxables, 1735–99, Pasquotank County Records; Tax Lists in County Settlements with the State, Treasurers and Comptrollers Papers; Tax Lists, 1720–1839, in Secretary of State Papers; Tax Lists, 1771–74, Legislative Papers, North Carolina State Archives.

Estimates for the years 1748 to 1755 were made for the Upper Cape Fear region by multiplying the 1763–71 percentage of slaves for the region for each category by the provincial average or the average percentage of slaves for each category within each of the five regions for which records exist for 1748 to 1755. The result was then divided by the provincial average or the average percentage of slaves for each category for all seven regions for the years 1763 to 1771. The number lower or greater than 100 was added or subtracted in accordance

of the degree to which slaves were concentrated on large plantations in North Carolina, Maryland, and Virginia perhaps leads to surprising results. In two tidewater counties in Maryland and one in Virginia, ca. 1750, an average of 60.8 percent of the slaves lived on plantations with eleven or more slaves and 32.7 percent on units with twenty-one or more slaves. In contrast, in all of North Carolina's regions the percentages of slaves living on plantations with ten or more slaves and twenty or more slaves were, respectively, 50.7 and 19.4. About twenty years later the differences between the Chesapeake region and North Carolina had decreased. The percentages of slaves on units of eleven or more and twenty-one or more in the former area were 67.7 and 36.3, while comparable percentages for all of North Carolina were 61.6 and 28.5.[14]

Since we have compared all of North Carolina's counties with

---

with the 1763–71 distribution in the Upper Cape Fear Region. A similar procedure was used to obtain estimates for the Central Inner Plain–Piedmont region for the years 1748 to 1755.

Estimates for North Carolina were obtained by using the following formula for each category (1 to 4 slaves, etc.):

$$y = \frac{xt + x_1t_1 + x_2t_2 + x_3t_3 + x_4t_4 + x_5t_5 + x_6t_6}{100}$$

Where:

y is the percentage of slaves within each category for each time period for the province; x, x_1, etc., is the percentage of slaves for each particular region for each category for each time period; t, t_1, etc., is the percentage of the province's slaves living within each particular region for each time period.

Data for the Albemarle Sound region for the early period consist of tax lists for Bertie County, 1751, and Pasquotank County, 1748. For the late period they consist of tax lists for Bertie County, 1768, and Pasquotank County, 1769. These tended to be average Albemarle Sound counties. Chowan County, for example, had more pronounced slaveholding features, as may be seen in the following statistics for Chowan in 1770: 1 to 4 slaves, 15.7 percent; 5 to 9 slaves, 18.0 percent; 10 to 19 slaves, 36.2 percent; 20 or more slaves, 30.1 percent.

Data for the Neuse-Pamlico region for the early period consist of a tax list for Beaufort County, 1755; for the later period tax lists for Beaufort-Pitt counties, 1764, and Onslow County, 1771, were used. Data for the Lower Cape Fear region consist of tax lists for New Hanover County, 1755 and 1767, and Brunswick County, 1769. Data for the Upper Cape Fear region consist of a tax list for Bladen County, 1763. (See earlier notation for methodology used to obtain a statement for the earlier period for this region.) Data for the Central Inner Plain–Piedmont region consist of tax lists for Pitt County, 1764, and Dobbs County, 1769. Data for the Northern Inner Plain–Piedmont region consist of two tax lists for Granville County, 1755 and 1769, and a tax list for Bute County, 1771. Data for the Western region consist of tax lists for Orange County, 1755, and Anson County, 1763.

only three tidewater counties in Maryland and Virginia, it is reasonable to assume that the estimates for the Chesapeake colonies overstate the actual concentrations of slaves on large production units for the two provinces. It is impossible to determine by how much, but probably the disparity between North Carolina and the Chesapeake colonies was considerably less than indicated above for the earlier period and of negligible importance or nonexistent for the later period. These demographic findings are significant, for they suggest that by the 1750s, and increasingly thereafter, slaves in North Carolina, at least in the east, were sufficiently concentrated on large units of production to provide for substantial social contact and close personal relationships.[15]

Sex ratios among North Carolina's slaves tell a similar story. By the period 1751 to 1755 sex ratios were between 137 and 163 males per 100 females in all regions of the province except in the Central Inner Plain–Piedmont, 182, the Upper Cape Fear, 188, and the west, 194 (see Table 3-6). Evidence uncovered by other investigators indicates that African slavers typically carried to Virginia about two male slaves for every female slave.[16] Probably a similar sex ratio existed among slaves brought directly from Africa to North Carolina. Since a large percentage of North Carolina's slave immigrants were both Creole and African-born slaves reexported from other colonies, however, the ratio of men to women among such slaves very likely was lower than that for slaves imported directly from Africa. This variable, in turn, beclouds the statistical role played by natural increase both in explaining growth-rate patterns among North Carolina's slaves, which we have discussed previously, and the interrelated factor of decreasing sex ratios.[17] Thus, North Carolina's sex ratios up to 1755 can possibly be explained largely by the immigration patterns peculiar to the colony.

Still, it is reasonable to assume that during the years after 1755 natural increase, along with a fast-growing Creole slave population, played an increasingly significant role in explaining the rapidly decreasing ratio of men to women among North Carolina's slave population. And this decrease occurred despite an increased flow of slaves into North Carolina from Africa and other colonies during these years. Thus, by the years 1761 to 1764 (and probably

Table 3-6. *Sample Slave Taxable Populations of North Carolina and Its Regions and Sex Ratios, 1751–1772*

Regions	1751–55 N Slave Tax- ables and Sex Ratios (males per 100 females)	1761–64 N Slave Tax- ables and Sex Ratios (males per 100 females)	1766–72 N Slave Tax- ables and Sex Ratios (males per 100 females)
Albemarle Sound Region[a]	1,642 163	—	10,109 134
Neuse-Pamlico Region[b]	1,755 143	—	3,238 121
Lower Cape Fear Region[c]	2,790 144	6,657 123	3,894 117
Upper Cape Fear Region[d]	346 188	667 129	—
Central Inner Plain– Piedmont Region[e]	168 182	883 128	—
Northern Inner Plain– Piedmont Region[f]	2,618 137	—	—
Western Region[g]	274 194	68 106	—
North Carolina (weighted estimates of ratios)	153	125	

Sources and Methods: Each extant county tax list that breaks down the county's taxable slave population by sex was used to determine the sex ratios in the above table. These tax lists are listed in the notes to the table. Since the slave taxable population was used to determine sex ratios, the slave population under twelve years of age has been ignored in these calculations.

Extant tax lists that noted the sex of slaves existed for the following regions and counties: Albemarle Sound—Bertie (1751, 1754, 1761, 1763, 1766, 1768, 1769, 1770, 1772), Chowan (1768, 1771), Currituck (1752, 1754), Pasquotank (1754, 1769), Perquimans (1771, 1772); Neuse-Pamlico—Beaufort (1754), Craven (1754, 1769), Hyde (1754), Onslow (1754, 1769, 1770, 1771); Lower Cape Fear—Brunswick (1764, 1769, 1772), New Hanover (1754, 1755, 1762, 1763, 1764, 1767); Upper Cape Fear—Bladen (1754, 1763); Central Inner Plain–Piedmont—Johnston (1763), Duplin (1754, 1762); Northern Inner Plain–Piedmont—Edgecombe (1754), Granville, (1754, 1755), Northampton (1754); Western—Anson (1754, 1763), Orange (1754, 1755), Rowan (1754).

Sex ratios for each region were obtained in the following manner. The actual sex ratios for the counties where data exist were weighted in accordance with the approximate number of blacks living in the county during the years surveyed (see Table 3-1). Thus, for the years 1751–54, estimates for 1755 were used; for 1761–64 and 1766–72, estimates for 1767 were used. If a county had sex ratio data for more than one year, an arithmetical mean was used to determine the county's sex ratio for the period involved. Lastly, we extrapolated for the Central Inner Plain–Piedmont and Western regions to achieve more representative samples. That is, we estimated mathematical trends in sex ratios for those counties where figures existed for two or more time periods and used these trends as multipliers to project probable trends in the counties for which we have actual sex ratios for at least one of the time periods.

North Carolina's sex ratios were calculated by using similar weighting techniques. To increase the sample, however, we conjoined the last two periods. Since there appears to have been little change in sex ratios over the years 1761–72, little distortion occurred by using this process.

The formula used to obtain a sex ratio is: $\dfrac{M}{F}$ k

Where:

M is the number of males recorded in some statistical universe of persons (North Carolina or a particular region); F is the number of females in the same universe; and k is an arbitrary factor of 100. For an informative analysis of sex ratios see George W. Barclay, *Techniques of Population Analysis* (New York: John Wiley and Sons, 1958), pp. 21–24.

We wish to thank Karl Vezner for devising the SAS computer programs necessary to construct this table.

a. Saunders, ed., *Colonial Records*, 5:320; Taxes and Accounts, 1679–1754, Colonial Court Records; Taxables, 1755–64, 1765–71, 1772–84; County Accounts, 1741–1860, Bertie County Records; County Settlements with the State, Tax Lists, Treasurers and Comptrollers Papers; Taxables, 1762–78, Chowan County Records; Lists of Taxables, Militia, and Magistrates, 1754–70, and undated, in Governors Office Papers; Tax Lists, 1720–1839, in Secretary of State Papers; List of Taxables, 1743–1836, Perquimans County Records; Tax Lists, 1771–74, in Legislative Papers, North Carolina State Archives.

b. Saunders, ed., *Colonial Records*, 5:320; Tax Lists, 1720–1839, in Secretary of State Papers; Tax Lists, 1771–74, in Legislative Papers, North Carolina State Archives.

c. Saunders, ed., *Colonial Records*, 5:320; Lists of Taxables, Militia, and Mag-

earlier) the ratios of men to women had decreased in the different regions for which we have data to a range of from 106 to 134 men per 100 women. These ratios, roughly averaging 125, remained stable through the early 1770s (see Table 3-6). The ratios of men to women, we can suppose, were low enough sometime after 1755, therefore, to enable large numbers of slaves to construct marital and familial patterns.

But slaves, of course, faced enormous problems in gradually overcoming not only difficult ecological conditions but also harsh laws and treatment in their quest to establish marriage and the family as well as other institutions and thereby at least partially to shape their own destinies in America. The attempt to implement that portion of their memories synthesized from a varied African past and integrated with new forms borrowed from or demanded by their American environment was still in process in North Carolina between 1750 and 1775—indeed as it would be throughout the history of slavery, in North Carolina and elsewhere. The question that can be asked for any given moment is "What was the distinctive dynamic, at that time, of Afro-American culture formation?" And, as we develop in other investigations, the answer with respect to marriage and the family in North Carolina during the years 1750 to 1775 varied depending on the size of plantation, the region, and the decade reviewed. Briefly, the process was well under way in the east during these years, while in the west, save on the largest slaveholdings, the process was in an early stage.[18]

istrates, 1754–70, and undated, in Governors Office Papers; Tax Lists, 1720–1839, in Secretary of State Papers; Tax Lists, 1771–74, in Legislative Papers; County Settlements with the State, Tax Lists, Treasurers and Comptrollers Papers, North Carolina State Archives.

d. Saunders, ed., *Colonial Records*, 5:320; Tax Lists, 1720–1839, in Secretary of State Papers, North Carolina State Archives.

e. Saunders, ed., *Colonial Records*, 5:320; Lists of Taxables, Militia, and Magistrates, 1754–70, and undated, in Governors Office Papers, North Carolina State Archives.

f. Saunders, ed., *Colonial Records*, 5:320; County Settlements with the State, Tax Lists, Treasurers and Comptrollers Papers, North Carolina State Archives.

g. Saunders, ed., *Colonial Records*, 5:320; County Settlements with the State, Tax Lists, Treasurers and Comptrollers Papers; Tax Lists, 1720–1839, in Secretary of State Papers, North Carolina State Archives.

Simply to use sex ratios as a gauge of sexual numerical imbalances, moreover, is significantly to understate the actual imbalances confronting slaves on plantations in colonial North Carolina and undoubtedly elsewhere as well. Sex ratios determined the maximum possible number of marriages that might occur in a given area at any given moment, and these ratios ultimately did affect family formation and population growth patterns. But sexual imbalances caused by sex ratios could be, and certainly were in colonial North Carolina, exaggerated further by a maldistribution of the slaves induced by the length of time a region was settled, the available supply of slaves, and the conscious choices made by masters. Both sex ratios and imbalance ratios must, therefore, be constructed.[19]

In an attempt to accomplish this it was necessary to use a different universe than the one used in Table 3-6 to develop sex ratios. Estate records (wills and inventories) for the years 1750 to 1775 were used to construct Table 3-7 instead of the tax records that were analyzed for Table 3-6. The resulting regional sex ratios for Tables 3-6 and 3-7, unfortunately, are not identical, although only the ratios for the interior regions, especially the west, are significantly at variance for the two tables. Though hardly satisfactory, one explanation for these variations is that the tax records concern slave taxables (slaves twelve years and over), while data gathered from wills and inventories is for adult slaves—sixteen years of age and older. Perhaps a more important explanation relates to the relative adequacy of the samples—Table 3-6 being constructed from more expansive samples.[20]

However aberrant some of the sex ratios constructed from the estate records might be, it is questionable if these aberrations significantly distort the differences in the sex imbalances measured by sex ratios and the actual distribution of slaves on the various plantations in each region. In Table 3-7 both sex ratios and imbalance ratios were used to calculate the percentages of slaves who could not be paired in marriage. Because these percentages may be visualized more readily, the ensuing discussion will focus upon them instead of the ratios from which they were derived. What is being compared and contrasted, then, are the calculated percentages of slaves who could not possibly marry because of regional sex ratios and the percentage of slaves who could not possibly marry given the sexual imbalances that actually existed on each plantation in each region.[21] In the latter case the effects of slavery itself upon the distribution of slaves by sex and age are taken into consideration. As previously suggested, many factors would play a role in causing the latter maldistribution, none of which can be discretely quantified: the slave trade, the length of time a region had been settled, the purchasing practices of masters, the inclination of owners to stress productive needs over reproductive needs, for example, and demands for particular slaves as they varied according to differences in the economy or the jobs slaves had to perform.

Table 3-7 illustrates that despite significant regional variations slavery itself exaggerated the impact of slave sex ratios throughout the province; that is, for whatever reason, slavery itself maldistributed slaves by sex considerably beyond what one would predict from regional sex ratios. For instance, in the Albemarle Sound region the possible percentage of slaves who could not be paired because of sex ratios equaled only 6.16 percent, while the percentage who could not be paired because of the actual sexual maldistribution on the different units of production was 30.04 percent (see Table 3-7).

Although the differences between the percentages calculated from imbalance ratios and the percentages calculated from sex ratios varied among the regions, the actual disparities are greater in the western regions than in those to the east (see Table 3-7)—that is, the further west one goes, the greater the actual sexual imbalances on particular plantations and the higher the proportion of slaves unable to marry other slaves on the home plantations because of a maldistribution of slaves by sex. In the three eastern regions from 30 to 39.3 percent of the slaves could not marry slaves on their own plantations because of sex disparities; in the two middle regions the percentages were slightly under 48 percent and 50 percent, while in the west it was fully 62 percent. Such percentages undoubtedly were further exaggerated by the many relatives slaves often had on the plantation on which they lived. Given the incest taboos and exogamous marital practices of slaves, these relationships would increase the percentage of slaves

Table 3-7. *Percentages of Adult Slaves Who Could Not Be Paired by Sex in Accordance with Sex Ratios as Compared with the Percentage of Adult Slaves Who Could Not Be Paired by Sex in Accordance with Imbalance Ratios (calculated for six of North Carolina's seven regions), 1748–1772*

Region	N Slave-holders/ Slaves	Adult Sex Ratios	Percentage of Adult Slaves Who Could Not Be Paired According to Sex Ratios	Adult Imbal- ance Ratios	Percentage of Adult Slaves Who Could Not Be Paired According to Imbalance Ratios
Albemarle Sound Region	79 243	113.16	6.17	53.80	30.04
Neuse-Pamlico Region	23 56	124.00	10.71	43.59	39.29
Lower Cape Fear Region	29 104	153.66	21.15	44.44	38.46
Central Inner Plain– Piedmont Region	9 12	200.0	33.33	33.33	50.00
Northern Inner Plain– Piedmont Region	19 42	162.50	23.81	35.48	47.62
Western Region	59 74	60.87	24.32	23.33	62.16

Sources and Methods: Wills and inventories from the following counties were used to arrive at the above statistics: Albemarle Sound region—Bertie and Pasquotank counties; Neuse-Pamlico region—Beaufort and Carteret counties; Lower Cape Fear region—Brunswick and New Hanover counties; Central Inner Plain–Piedmont region—Cumberland County; Northern Inner Plain–Piedmont region—Northampton and Halifax counties; Western region—Anson, Mecklenburg, Orange, and Rowan counties. These wills and inventories are in the following collections in the North Carolina State Archives: Secretary of State's Records—North Carolina Wills, 1663–1789, S.S. 845–873, vols. 7–35; Chancery Proceedings and Wills, 1712–54, S.S. 878; Wills, 1738–52, 1750–58, 1755–58, 1758–73, S.S. 877, 879–81, vols. 4, 6–8; Inventories and Sales of Estates, 1714–98, S.S. 889–905. Bertie County Wills, C.R. 10.801.1–10.801.8,

vols. 1–8; Bertie County Estates Papers, C.R. 10.504.1–10.504.1.15, C.R.
10.504.1.19–10.504.1.114; Bertie County, Inventories of Estates, C.R.
10.507.2. Carteret County Records, Miscellaneous Papers, 1717–1844, Book A,
Records of Wills and Bonds, C.R. 19.905.1; Wills, Inventories, Sales, and Settlement of Estates, C.R. 19.802.1–19.802.11, vols. 1–11; Carteret County Wills,
C.R. 19.801.1, 19.905.1. New Hanover Wills, C.R. vols. 105, C.R. 70.801.1–
70.801.5. Northampton County Wills, C.R. 71.801.1, 71.802.1, 71.802.2.
Cumberland County Wills, C.R. 29.801.1–29.801.4. Mecklenburg County
Wills, 1749–1869, C.R. 65.009–65.027; Estate Papers, C.R. 065 508.3–C.R.
065 508.140. Orange County Estates Papers, 1758–85, C.R. 73.507.1.

As we have seen in Table 3-5, in order to compute the sex ratio for the 218
holdings in the data under discussion, the procedure would be simply to total the
males and females separately over all holdings. With the resultant sum of males
and sum of females, the sex ratio is easily computed.

The "imbalance ratio," on the other hand, takes into account not only the ratio
of males to females but also the imbalance between their numbers that exists in
each holding. It treats each holding as if it were a closed unit in terms of marital
relationships. The imbalance ratio is a ratio of the number of the gender in the
minority to the number of the gender in the majority in a holding. As one moves
from the data from one holding to the data from another holding, the two totals
that are incremented are the number in the minority and the number in the majority. In keeping with the sex ratio, the resulting ratio is multiplied by 100.

For example, suppose that there were four holdings that had the following distribution of gender for adults: (1) 1 male; (2) 1 female; (3) 5 males and 3 females; and (4) 5 females and 3 males. The overall sex ratio would, of course, be
100, as there are the same number of males and females. The imbalance ratio,
however, would be computed as follows:

Holding	Minority Gender	Majority Gender
1	0 (female)	1 (male)
2	0 (male)	1 (female)
3	3 (female)	5 (male)
4	3 (male)	5 (female)
Total	6	12

The imbalance ratio would be (6/12)100 or 50, a far cry from the sex ratio of
100. To the extent that individual holdings were closed units, the imbalance ratio
is much to be preferred in that it more closely approximates reality.

The same example can be used to illustrate the computation of a related
statistic that is more easily grasped: the percent of adults who cannot be paired
with an adult of the opposite sex. Each of the six in the minority gender column
can be paired with an adult of the opposite sex in the majority gender column.
Thus, a total of twelve can be paired with a member of the opposite sex, leaving
six in the majority column who cannot be paired. The six are 33.3 percent of the
total of eighteen slaves, which is the percent of nonpaired adults.

unable to find mates on their own plantations. On the other hand, to the degree that interplantation marriages occurred, and this was probably with some frequency, they alleviated the problems caused by sex imbalances on particular plantations.

But whatever the effects of these last factors, it is reasonable to conclude that even given the strongest will on the part of the slaves and the complete cooperation of masters, a goodly majority of the slaves in the west simply could not marry persons on their own plantations, and, therefore, most western slaves were not members of double-headed households during the years 1750 to 1775. Such marriages and households were, of course, more common to the eastward. It is also quite probable that the double-headed family in North Carolina, while strongly desired by slaves and significantly implemented by them, was still in the process of becoming the definitive familial mode that historian Herbert Gutman argues existed for the antebellum period and that Kulikoff suggests had been manifested by the 1750s in the Chesapeake.[22]

Finally, by using the sex ratios in Table 3-6 and fitting them within Kulikoff's findings for the Chesapeake region, perhaps a reasonably close estimate of the number of African slaves residing in North Carolina may be made. Kulikoff suggests that "if the entire population (of a colonial area) were African, the sex ratio would be about 200; when a third of the adults were Afro-Ameri-

---

The percent of nonpaired adults can also be computed directly from the imbalance ratio using the following formula:

$$100 \left(\frac{100 - \text{Imbalance Ratio}}{100 + \text{Imbalance Ratio}} \right) = 100 \left(\frac{100 - 50}{100 + 50} \right) = 33.3$$

The percent of nonpaired adults can be computed directly from the sex ratio by using the following formula when sex ratio is greater than 100:

$$\frac{\text{Sex Ratio} - 100}{\text{Sex Ratio} + 100} = \frac{113.16 - 100}{113.16 + 100} = 6.17$$

When sex ratio is less than 100 the formula would be:

$$\frac{100 - \text{Sex Ratio}}{100 + \text{Sex Ratio}} = \frac{100 - 60.87}{100 + 60.87} = 24.32$$

cans, the sex ratio would drop to 156"; and if "Africans constituted only a third of the adult population, the sex ratio would decline to 125."[23]

Kulikoff's estimates suggest that Africans made up about two-thirds of North Carolina's adult slave population between 1751 and 1755, when sex ratios averaged around 153, and about a third during the last fifteen years of the colonial period, when sex ratios averaged about 125. These findings, in turn, support previous assertions that the percentage of Africans in the province's black population dramatically decreased from 1751 to 1761 and that, despite a heavy inflow of immigrants from the latter year to 1772, the percentage of Africans in the colony's slave population remained stable during these last twelve years. More important, the heavy influx of Africans during the last twenty-five years of the colonial period and the fact that on the average they made up about half the adult population during the years 1750 to 1772 ensured that African cultural characteristics exerted a powerful influence over slaves and, by means of cultural diffusion, affected whites as well.

The presence of numerous Africans with active memories of and experiences in their homeland significantly contributed, therefore, to the development of an Afro-American culture in colonial North Carolina. To assert the importance of African memories in this case is to argue the role of the experiential, which is another way of asserting the importance of the habitual. However much slavery and whites inhibited an African continuum and however much an insistent present demanded dynamic cultural change to meet new or changing circumstances, these forces probed, clashed, and interacted with the past African experiences of the slaves.

The experiential, therefore—that which constantly evoked conscious or unthinking but essentially organic modes of comprehension and behavior—was ultimately African. And though varied and fragmented, this African experience was transmitted to the first generation of slaves born in America, who in turn entered the cultural dynamic as active participants with their own African-rooted values, needs, and sense of reality. African and Creole worlds thus continued the process of interpenetration with a frequently hostile European culture that placed severe if not always consistent restrictions on slaves and subjected them to fluctuating epidemiological and demographic conditions.

A dynamic process so complex and multifaceted presents an extraordinary challenge to historians who wish to reconstruct and comprehend it. Even under the best of scholarly conditions the task would be difficult, but when there is a dearth of data, it often becomes impossible to reach beyond conjecture or a sketchy outline. The African relationship, nonetheless, is one that can and must be pursued.[24]

Authorities on free blacks in the South present some estimates but no statistical data concerning the size of this group in North Carolina before 1790.[25] Nevertheless, historian Ira Berlin's estimate has proven surprisingly accurate. Noting that a Maryland census of 1755 reveals that free blacks equaled 4 percent of that colony's total black population and that North Carolina's percentage of free blacks was 4.7 in 1790 despite the dislocations of the Revolution, he estimates the late-colonial free black population in the latter province to be about 4 percent of that colony's total black population. This estimate is a bit more than 1 percent less than the percentage indicated by the data we have collected (see Tables 3-8 to 3-10).[26]

The relative size of the free black population, however, varied greatly among the regions of North Carolina. In older, more mature coastal regions smaller proportions of the black populations were free than in later developing more westerly regions. This was especially true of the Lower Cape Fear, where blacks were most densely populated and were overwhelmingly concentrated on large production units. Free blacks in this region made up only about 1 percent of the black population, a strong indication that demographic and economic conditions tended to limit at least one of the following: the manumission of slaves, the rate at which white females bore mulatto children, and the capacity of free blacks to remain in the region. The considerably higher percentages of free blacks in the two other coastal regions coincide with a lesser proportion of blacks in the total populations, a lower black population density, and a lighter concentration of slaves on large

Table 3-8. *Estimates from Tax Records Concerning the Numbers of Taxables Who Were Slaves, Free Whites, Free Blacks (Mulattoes)–Black (Mulatto) Servants, and White Servants*

County	Year	White Taxables	Free White Taxables	White Servant Taxables
Beaufort[a]	1755	758	676	82
Cumberland[b]	1755	293	267	26
Granville[c]	1755	824	785	39
			700	124
New Hanover[d]	1755	396	—	—
Orange[e]	1755	983	—	—
Cumberland[f]	1762	626	—	—
Anson[g]	1763	428	—	—
Bertie[h]	1763	794	633	161
Cumberland[i]	1763	652	632	20
Beaufort-Pitt[j]	1764	1,115	991	124
Bertie[k]	1766	761	—	—
Cumberland[l]	1767	896	—	—
New Hanover[m]	1767	514	—	—
Bertie[n]	1768	806	596	210
Bertie[o]	1769	885	—	—
Brunswick[p]	1769	260	—	—
Granville[q]	1769	1,104	—	—
Pasquotank[r]	1769	974	912	62

a. County Settlements with the State, Tax Lists, Treasurers and Comptrollers Papers, North Carolina State Archives.
b. Ibid.
c. Ibid.
d. Ibid.
e. Ibid.
f. Lists of Taxables, Militia, and Magistrates, 1754–70, in Governors Office Papers, North Carolina State Archives.
g. Tax Lists, 1720–1839, in Secretary of State Papers, North Carolina State Archives.
h. Taxables, 1755–64, Bertie County Records, North Carolina State Archives.
i. Lists of Taxables, Militia, and Magistrates, 1754–70, in Governors Office Papers.

Black-Mulatto Servants or Free Persons (taxables)	Slave Taxables		Total Taxables
	Male	Female	
36	568		1,362
11	61		365
35	223	211	1,293
9	841	572	1,818
20	75	35	1,113
20	172		818
7	38	44	517
51	446	430	1,721
—	201		873
36	794		1,945
54	487	445	1,747
11	350		1,257
32	794	678	2,018
34	539	485	1,861
63	611	565	2,124
8	657	584	1,509
63	971		2,138
10	770		1,754

Tax Lists, 1720–1839, in Secretary of State Papers, North Carolina State
chives.
Taxables, 1765–71, Bertie County Records, North Carolina State Archives.
County Settlements with the State, Tax Lists, Treasurers and Comptrollers Pa-
rs, North Carolina State Archives.
, Tax Lists, 1720–1839, in Secretary of State Papers, North Carolina State
rchives.
Taxables, 1765–71, Bertie County Records, North Carolina State Archives.
Ibid.
Tax Lists, 1720–1839, in Secretary of State Papers, North Carolina State
rchives.
Ibid.
Ibid.

Table 3-9. *Estimates from Tax Records Concerning the Numbers of Persons Who Were Slaves, Free Whites, Free Blacks (Mulattoes)–Black (Mulatto) Servants, and White Servants*

County	Year	Whites	Free Whites	White Servants
Beaufort	1755	3,108	2,772	336
Cumberland	1755	1,201	1,095	107
Granville	1755	3,378	3,219	160
			2,870	508
New Hanover	1755	1,624	——	——
Orange	1755	4,030	——	——
Cumberland	1762	2,567	——	——
Anson	1763	1,755	——	——
Bertie	1763	3,255	2,595	660
Cumberland	1763	2,673	2,591	82
Beaufort-Pitt	1764	4,572	4,063	508
Bertie	1766	3,120	——	——
Cumberland	1767	3,674	——	——
New Hanover	1767	2,107	——	——
Bertie	1768	3,305	2,444	861
Bertie	1769	3,629	——	——
Brunswick	1769	1,066	——	——
Granville	1769	4,526	——	——
Pasquotank	1769	3,993	3,739	254

plantations. These correlations generally hold true for the remainder of the colony (see Tables 3-8 to 3-10).

Since the relative size of the free black population is correlated with demographic characteristics and economic maturity of specific regions, this phenomenon may be traced over time *within* all of North Carolina's regions except the Lower Cape Fear. There

Black-Mulatto Servants or Free Persons	Slaves Males	Females	Totals
68	1,074		4,520
21	115		1,337
66	422	399	4,265
17	1,590	1,024	4,255
38	142	66	4,276
38	325		2,930
13	72	83	1,923
96	843	813	5,007
—	380		3,053
68	1,501		6,141
102	920	841	4,983
21	662		4,357
61	1,501	1,281	4,950
64	1,019	917	5,305
119	1,155	1,068	5,971
15	1,242	1,104	3,427
119	1,835		6,480
19	1,455		5,467

Note: Taxable figures from Table 3-8 were converted into the above population figures by using multipliers of 4.1 in white taxables and 1.89 on black taxables.

the germane demographic and economic characteristics remained quite stable during the years under investigation. As the other regions matured economically during the 1750s and 1760s, however, slaves became more numerous and concentrated, and the proportion of free blacks in the black population decreased. The patterns in Granville County, however, suggest that the drop in the

Table 3-10. *Comparative Analysis of Slave and Free Black Populations for Selected Counties, Regions, and Province, 1755–1769*

Regions and Counties	Year	Free Blacks N	Slaves N	Free Black Percentage of Black Population (mean percentage)
Albemarle Sound Region	1763–1769			3.79
Bertie	1763	96	1,656	5.48
Bertie[a]	1766	102	1,761	5.48 ⎫ 4.59
Bertie	1768	64	1,936	3.20 ⎭
Bertie	1769	119	2,223	5.08
Pasquotank	1769	19	1,455	1.29
Neuse-Pamlico Region	1755–1764			5.14
Beaufort	1755	68	1,074	5.95
Beaufort	1764	68	1,501	4.33
Lower Cape Fear Region	1755–1769			1.06
New Hanover	1755	17	2,614	.65
New Hanover and Brunswick	1767 ⎫ 1769 ⎭	76	5,128	1.46
Central Inner Plain–Piedmont Region	1755–1767			9.66
Cumberland	1755	21	115	15.44
Cumberland	1762	38	325	10.47
Cumberland	1767	21	662	3.07
Northern Inner Plain–Piedmont Region	1755–1769			6.77

Table 3-10. *(continued)*

Regions and Counties	Year	Free Blacks N	Slaves N	Free Black Percentage of Black Population (mean percentage)
Granville	1755	66	821	7.44
Granville	1769	119	1,835	6.09
West	1755–1763			11.60
Orange	1755	38	208	15.45
Anson	1763	13	155	7.74
North Carolina[b] (weighted estimate)	1755–1769			5.35

Note: Figures for Table 3-9 deal with population (not taxable) totals. The statistics were abstracted from Table 3-8.

a. The arithmetical mean percentage for Bertie County for the years 1766, 1768, and 1769—4.59—was used together with the mean percentages for Bertie, 1763, and Pasquotank, 1769, to calculate the mean percentage for the Albemarle.

b. Free black percentage for North Carolina was obtained by weighting each region's free blacks percentage in accordance with the percentage of the province's blacks living in each region. Percentage in this case equals the mean percentage listed in Table 3-2 for each region for years 1755 and 1767.

proportion of free blacks lagged somewhat behind the rise in related economic and demographic characteristics (see Tables 3-1, 3-2, 3-3, 3-5, and 3-10).

Clearly, then, a positive correlation existed between the newness of settlement and limited economic maturation and the presence of relatively large numbers of free blacks during the period 1748 to 1772. In the earlier years the scarcity of labor and limited numbers of slaves dictated a comparatively adventuresome use of different types of labor: free persons, servants, and slaves. De-

spite increasing fears and taboos and ever more restrictive legislation the status of such diverse laborers during the early years of
development was less directly related to color than would be the
case in the later years, as the province grew in economic maturity.
As economic growth occurred, the demand for slaves increased
faster than the demand for other dependent laborers, leading to a
disproportionately enlarged slave population that was increasingly
concentrated in the hands of wealthy planters. In addition, and
both a consequence and cause of the growth of slave numbers
discussed above, tolerance levels for manumission, miscegena-
tion (except probably among female slaves and whites), and the
presence of free blacks very likely all diminished. The limited
documentary evidence, therefore, suggests that the proportion of
free persons in the black population dwindled during the last
twenty-five years North Carolina remained a colony. Even the
dislocations of the Revolution probably did little or nothing to
reverse this tendency.[27]

Berlin's assertion that the southern free black population during
the colonial period was made up largely of mulattoes was probably true for North Carolina.[28] Certainly the province's tax collectors asserted as much when they used the term "mulattoes" inter-
changeably with those of "free negroes" and "free blacks." In so
doing, of course, the tax collectors also subsumed probably the
greatest number of mulattoes, those born of slave mothers, under
the tax designations "slaves" and "blacks."[29]

Most free blacks were mulattoes for a variety of reasons. First,
probably a disproportionately large number of those slaves who
were manumitted were mulattoes. Second, ex-slaves intermarried
with whites to avoid deportation or a return to bondage.[30] Third,
illegitimate children born to white women and black fathers—
slaves, servants, or freemen—were legally free. Lastly, free
blacks (mostly mulattoes) increased naturally, with some of the
children being fathered by white men.[31]

Some of the province's mulatto births were recorded in the
county court minutes as court orders binding out illegitimate mulatto children and, perchance, punishing their mothers. A review
of such documents reveals that many, but not all, of the mulatto
children of white servant mothers were placed in servitude until

the age of thirty-one, as provincial law directed. The records also indicate that children placed in servitude until this age, instead of the usual age of twenty-one for males or eighteen for females, were always mulatto children born of white servant mothers, except for an occasional nonwhite child born of a mulatto or black servant mother.[32] In accordance with statutory law, the white servant mothers who bore mulatto children were frequently ordered by the county courts to serve an extra two years beyond their original terms of indenture for each mulatto child to whom they gave birth. Also in keeping with statutory law, there is no evidence that mothers who were black or mulatto servants and bore children out of wedlock were ever bound out by the county courts for periods longer than one year for each child.[33]

A survey of the county court minutes also indicates that a considerable number of *free* white women had mulatto children out of wedlock, but that these women, in accordance with the law of 1741, did not automatically serve terms of indenture, although some, because of their poverty, eventually became servants. Moreover, poverty or possibly at times the preference of some free white mothers not to raise their mulatto children resulted in the binding out of many of these children—but never to the age of thirty-one. Apprenticed or indentured mulatto male children of free mothers (white, mulatto, or black) were treated similarly to their male white counterparts, being bound out until the age of twenty-one. On the other hand, when mulatto female minors whose mothers were free were bound out, they were at times discriminated against, whatever the color of their mothers, by being indentured or apprenticed until the age of twenty-one. White female minors were almost always bound out until eighteen, except for a few girls who were bound out to the age of sixteen.[34]

Berlin's belief that the origins of the free black population are largely explained by the incidence of mulatto children born out of wedlock to white mothers cannot be confirmed for North Carolina. While extant records document many more such births than they document manumissions, inadequate data make it impossible to come up with firm statistical statements. Yet the documents do strongly indicate a more general point, that children born out of wedlock to free and servant white, mulatto, and black mothers were fairly numerous and that these mothers and children normally all shared the pain of poverty, powerlessness, exploitation, and public ignominy.[35]

This discussion of the free black population necessarily introduces the question of apprenticeship and servitude in colonial North Carolina. It is certain that servants were always an important source of labor in the colony, even though by 1748 they had become less numerous than slaves. Important regional and temporal variations occurred during the years 1748 to 1772, however, for servants seem to have been relatively more numerous in the less economically mature regions and consequently somewhat less significant in the 1770s than in the 1750s (see Tables 3-8, 3-9, 3-11).

Recognizing an indeterminate margin of error in our statistical analysis, it is nonetheless quite certain that free blacks, generally poor and subjected to severe tax discrimination, were as a group in considerably greater danger of being placed in servitude than were whites.[36] This tendency increased over time, for it also appears to have been positively correlated with regional economic maturity and the length of time a region had been settled. We have found, for instance, that the proportion of free blacks who were servants in the Albemarle region was about eight to nine times greater than was the case among whites. The Neuse-Pamlico region had a similar ratio, while the Lower Cape Fear region had a ratio of about 9.5 to 1. On the other hand, the Western and Northern Inner Plain–Piedmont regions, respectively, had ratios that were between 3 and 4 to 1 (see Tables 3-12, 3-13).

The same factors that disproportionately forced free blacks into servitude at times also resulted in their illegal enslavement. Poverty, low social status, relative political powerlessness, legal limitations upon manumission, discriminatory legislation against free blacks, and fear among whites of free blacks as an anomaly and a focal point for slave rebellions all made free blacks vulnerable to the aggressions of unscrupulous whites intent upon enslaving them for profit. The numerical importance of this phenomenon is unclear, but a number of cases involving blacks who challenged their illegal enslavements are recorded in various county court minutes. Since it is likely that most blacks subjected to such

Table 3-11. *Comparative Analysis of White Servant and Slave Populations in Some Counties and Regions and the Province, 1755–1769*

Regions and Counties	Year	White Servants N	Slaves N	Ratio of Slave Population to Servant Population (approximate)[a]	Servant Percentage of Unfree Population
Albemarle Sound Region	1763–69	1,755	5,047	3:1	26.02
Bertie	1763	660	1,656		28.50
Bertie	1768	861	1,936		30.85 } 22.86
Pasquotank	1769	254	1,455		14.86 }
Neuse-Pamlico Region	1755–64	844	2,575	3:1	24.69
Beaufort	1755	336	1,074		23.83
Beaufort-Pitt	1764	508	1,501		25.29
Central Inner Plain–Piedmont Region	1755–63	195	495	2.5:1	28.26
Cumberland	1755	107	115		48.20
Cumberland	1763	82	380		17.75
Northern Inner Plain–Piedmont Region					
Granville	1755	160	821	5:1	16.31
		508		1.5:1	38.22
North Carolina— Mean of Regional Means	1755–69			3.5:1	23.82
				2:1	29.30

Note: Figures for Table 3-11 deal with population (not taxable) totals. The statistics were abstracted from Table 3-9.

a. Precise ratios for each region are: Albemarle Sound Region—5.05:1.78; Neuse-Pamlico Region—2.58:0.84; Central Inner Plain–Piedmont Region—4.95:1.95; Northern Inner Plain–Piedmont Region—5:1 and 1.5:1; North Carolina—5.2:1.54 and 5.2:2.41.

Table 3-12. *Racial and Sexual Distribution of Servants in Eleven Sample Counties in Five Regions during the Years 1748 to 1772 Who Were Bound Out Until They Reached Their Majority— Eighteen to Thirty-one Years of Age*

| Regions and Counties | Whites | | Nonwhites | | Total | |
	Males (number & percentage)	Females (number & percentage)	Males (number & percentage)	Females (number & percentage)	Whites (number & percentage)	Nonwhites (number & percentage)
Albemarle	290	62	38	38	352	76
Sound Region[a]	82.4	17.6	50.0	50.0	82.2	17.8
Pasquotank	57	18	1	8	75	9
County	76.0	24.0	11.1	88.9	89.3	10.7
Chowan	137	25	11	3	162	14
County	84.5	15.5	78.6	11.4	92.0	8.0
Bertie	96	19	26	27	115	53
County	83.5	16.5	49.1	50.9	68.5	31.5
Neuse-Pamlico	176	32	34	34	208	68
Region[b]	84.6	15.4	50.9	50.9	75.4	24.6
Beaufort	13	4	4	1	17	5
County	76.5	23.5	80.0	20.0	77.3	22.7
Craven	128	21	20	15	149	35
County	85.9	14.1	57.1	42.9	81.0	19.0
Carteret	35	7	10	18	42	28
County	83.3	16.7	35.7	64.3	60.0	40.0
Lower Cape Fear Region[c]						
New Hanover	14	11	2	3	25	5
County	56.0	44.0	60.0	40.0	83.3	16.7
Northern Inner Plain–Piedmont Region[d]						
Edgecombe	41	14	2	3	55	5
County	74.5	25.5	40.0	60.0	91.7	8.3
Western	81	52	0	3	133	3
Region[e]	60.9	39.1	0	100.0	97.8	2.2
Orange	35	20	0	1	55	1
County	63.6	36.4	0	100	98.2	1.8

Table 3-12. *(continued)*

Regions and Counties	Whites Males (number & percentage)	Whites Females (number & percentage)	Nonwhites Males (number & percentage)	Nonwhites Females (number & percentage)	Total Whites (number & percentage)	Total Nonwhites (number & percentage)
Rowan County	45	29	0	2	74	2
	60.8	39.2	0	100	97.4	2.6
Anson County	1	3	0	0	4	0
	25.0	75.0	0	0	100	0

Sources: These figures were obtained from an exhaustive analysis of the county court minutes in the North Carolina State Archives for each of the counties listed on Table 3-12.

a. Pasquotank County Court Minutes, 1738–72; Chowan County Court Minutes, 1748–72; Bertie County Court Minutes, 1758–72.

b. Beaufort County—Minutes, Appearance, Prosecution, and Trial Docket, Court of Pleas and Quarter Sessions, vol. 1, 1756–61; Craven County Court Minutes, 1750–72; Carteret County Court Minutes, 1748–72.

c. New Hanover County Court Minutes, 1748–69, 1771–72.

d. Edgecombe County Court Minutes, 1757–72.

e. Orange County Court Minutes, 1752–76; Rowan County—Minutes, Court of Pleas and Quarter Sessions, 1753–72; Anson County—Minute Docket of County Court plus Minutes, County Court of Pleas and Quarter Sessions, 1771–72.

treatment never brought their cases before the county courts, the existing records probably reveal only a relative few of the actual cases.[37]

As tragic as the consequences were to each free black illegally enslaved, such cases affected far more blacks than those specifically violated. Members of their families, friends, acquaintances, indeed all blacks, slave or free, who knew of the events were affected by them, just as blacks reacted to the sale or whipping of other slaves.[38] The message to all blacks was simple: most whites viewed free blacks as a dangerous aberration, and some were willing to use every available means to enslave them. Slavery, therefore, was all encompassing and permanent; freedom, but a temporary reprieve.

Blacks, slave or free, of course, refused to succumb totally to such a numbing fatalism. Documents reveal that free blacks of different counties and even different provinces collaborated to free kin, friends, and acquaintances who had been illegally en-

Table 3-13. *Estimates of the Ratio of Blacks Who Were Servants beyond a Projection of Their Population Totals in Selected Regions and the Province (one equals a projection of their population totals)*

Regions	Ratio
Albemarle Sound Region	8.64:1
Neuse-Pamlico Region	8.21:1
Lower Cape Fear Region	9.52:1
Northern Inner Plain–Piedmont Region	3.57:1
Western Region	3.17:1

Sources and Methods: For sources see notes to Table 3-11. The formula used to obtain the ratio (r) for each region is:

$$\frac{p}{\left(\dfrac{\dfrac{b_1}{w_1 + b_1} + \dfrac{b_2}{w_2 + b_2}}{2}\right) 100} = r$$

Where:

w_1 is the sum of the number of whites (Table 3-1) in each of the counties listed in Table 3-10 for a given region, ca. 1755.

w_2 is the same calculation for ca. 1767.

b_1 is the sum of the number of free blacks (Table 3-10) in each of the counties listed in Table 3-10 for a given region, ca. 1755.

b_2 is the same calculation for ca. 1767.

p is the percentage of all persons bound out until their majority (eighteen to thirty-one years of age) who were nonwhite within a particular region. This calculation involves using a different universe from that used to arrive at the previous calculations and consequently adds to the probability of error. The percentage used for each region equals the percentage listed in Table 3-12.

The above approximation formula makes use of disparate statistical information to arrive at an estimate of how frequently free blacks became servants in comparison with whites. This is accomplished because the numerator of the above formula is an estimate of the percent of servants who were nonwhites while the denominator equals an estimate of the percent of the population that was free black. If free blacks and whites became servants with equal frequency, the numerator and denominator would be equal and the ratio would equal one. Thus, to the degree the denominator is less than the numerator, free blacks disproportionately became servants.

slaved and that free blacks also joined together with sympathetic whites to prevent or correct these injustices.[39] Whatever the odds against success, whatever the frustrations or despair, blacks, free and slave, resisted the injustices consequent to enslavement, attempted to extend the boundaries of freedom, and challenged slavery itself.

NOTES

We wish to thank Jeffrey J. Crow, Flora J. Hatley, and the staff of the University of North Carolina Press for their competent and gracious aid as editors. It has been a pleasure working with them. We also wish to thank Karl Vezner, professor of political science, University of Toledo, for all his help in devising the formulas and computer programs necessary to implement Table 3-7, which deals with sex imbalance ratios. Lastly, we wish to express our appreciation to the director and staff of the North Carolina State Archives for their always thoughtful and competent cooperation.

1. An important exception is John Spencer Bassett, *Slavery and Servitude in the Colony of North Carolina*, Johns Hopkins University Studies in Historical and Political Science, ser. 14 (Baltimore: Johns Hopkins Press, 1896), pp. 27–61.

2. William L. Saunders, ed., *The Colonial Records of North Carolina*, 10 vols. (Raleigh: State of North Carolina, 1886–90), 1:720, 722, 2:xvii, 419; Evarts B. Greene and Virginia C. Harrington, *American Population before the Federal Census of 1790* (New York: Columbia University Press, 1932), p. 156.

3. Hugh Talmage Lefler and Albert Ray Newsome, *North Carolina: The History of a Southern State*, 3d ed. (Chapel Hill: University of North Carolina Press, 1973), pp. 43–75 passim; Hugh T. Lefler and William S. Powell, *Colonial North Carolina: A History* (New York: Scribner, 1973), pp. 43–88 passim; Jeffrey J. Crow, *The Black Experience in Revolutionary North Carolina* (Raleigh: Department of Cultural Resources, 1977), p. 4; Harry Roy Merrens, *Colonial North Carolina in the Eighteenth Century: A Study in Historical Geography* (Chapel Hill: University of North Carolina Press, 1964), pp. 18–31.

4. Saunders, ed., *Colonial Records*, 2:xvii, 3:433; Merrens, *Colonial North Carolina in the Eighteenth Century*, pp. 20–21.

5. Ian Charles Cargill Graham, *Colonists from Scotland: Emigration to North America, 1707–1783* (Ithaca: Cornell University Press, 1956),

pp. 94–96, 106, 108–9, 146, 154, 156, 157, 159–60; Duane Gilbert Meyer, "The Scottish Highlanders in North Carolina, 1773–1776," Ph.D. diss., University of Iowa, 1956, pp. 54–55, 90, 95, 97, 125, 128, 135; William K. Boyd, ed., *Some Eighteenth-Century Tracts Concerning North Carolina* (Raleigh: North Carolina Historical Commission, 1927), pp. 419–21; R. D. W. Connor, *Race Elements in the White Population of North Carolina* (Greensboro: North Carolina State Normal and Industrial College, 1920); William Herman Gehrke, "The German Element in Rowan and Cabarrus Counties," M.A. thesis, University of North Carolina, 1934, and "The Beginnings of the Pennsylvania German Element in Rowan and Cabarrus Counties, North Carolina," *Pennsylvania Magazine of History and Biography* 58, no. 4 (1934): 342–69; Lefler and Newsome, *North Carolina*, pp. 77–88; Lefler and Powell, *Colonial North Carolina*, pp. 88–108; Marvin L. Michael Kay, "The Institutional Background to the Regulation in Colonial North Carolina," Ph.D. diss., University of Minnesota, 1962, pp. 21–68; Merrens, *Colonial North Carolina in the Eighteenth Century*, pp. 53–107; American Council of Learned Societies, "Report of Committee on Linguistic and National Stocks in the Population of the United States," American Historical Association, *Annual Report for the Year 1931* (Washington, D.C., 1932), 1:107–441, but especially the table on pp. 124–25; Forrest McDonald and Ellen Shapiro McDonald, "The Ethnic Origins of the American People, 1790," *William and Mary Quarterly*, 3d ser., 37 (April 1980): 179–99. The growth patterns illustrated in Tables 3-1, 3-2, and 3-3 demonstrate the statement made in the text that the more westerly regions' population growth was partially the result of emigration from the Albemarle Sound and Neuse-Pamlico regions. See especially Table 3-3 and the yearly rate of growth patterns for these two regions.

6. Merrens in his excellent work asserts this. See *Colonial North Carolina in the Eighteenth Century*, pp. 79–81, 226 (n. 61). It is true, however, that the extant official records of slave entries into North Carolina's ports do support Merrens's contention. See the following, which Merrens cites on p. 226 (n. 61): Saunders, ed., *Colonial Records*, 3:430, 621, 5:314, 9:179; U.S. Bureau of the Census, *Historical Statistics of the United States: Colonial Times to 1957* (Washington, D.C., 1960), series Z 290, p. 769. Merrens further correctly points out that the most important collection of documents about the slave trade does not include a section dealing with North Carolina because the editor could find almost no evidence of slave imports into the province (Elizabeth Donnan, ed., *Documents Illustrative of the History of the Slave Trade to America*, 4 vols. [Washington, D.C.: Carnegie Institu-

tion of Washington, 1930–35], 4:235–36). Bassett also argues this position. See his *Slavery and Servitude*, pp. 22–23.

7. Allan Kulikoff, "Tobacco and Slaves: Population, Economy, and Society in Eighteenth-Century Prince George's County, Maryland," Ph.D. diss., Brandeis University, 1976, p. 84.

8. *North Carolina Magazine*, 7–14 and 21–28 September, 19–26 October 1764; John Brickell, *The Natural History of North Carolina with an Account of the Trade, Manners, and Customs of the Christian and Indian Inhabitants* (Dublin: James Carson, 1737; reprint ed., Raleigh: Trustees of the Public Libraries, 1911), p. 45. The advertisements in the *North Carolina Magazine* in three instances refer only to a "Parcel" of slaves. Twenty slaves were imported on the "Brig. CHANCE"; the estimate of fifty as the total is based on a conservative estimate that ten slaves arrived on each of the smaller vessels. None of the notices specifies the birthplace of the slaves. The *North Carolina Magazine*, 28 September–5 October 1764, did state that between 1 October 1763 and 1 October 1764 a total of 179 slaves were imported through Port Beaufort alone. This lends support to our assertion that the estimate of fifty for all the colony's ports for a two-month period is conservative.

9. Saunders, ed., *Colonial Records*, 3:430–33.

10. The above figures dealing with South Carolina were obtained by W. Robert Higgins in his research in the records of South Carolina and those of the British Public Records Office. He cordially shared these data with us by letter, and we wish to thank him.

11. W. Robert Higgins, "The Geographical Origins of Negro Slaves in Colonial South Carolina," *South Atlantic Quarterly* 70 (Winter 1971): 34–47; Philip D. Curtin, *The Atlantic Slave Trade: A Census* (Madison: University of Wisconsin Press, 1969), pp. 155–58; Darold D. Wax, "Preferences for Slaves in Colonial America," *Journal of Negro History* 58 (October 1973): 371–401.

12. Russell R. Menard, "The Maryland Slave Population, 1658 to 1730: A Demographic Profile of Blacks in Four Counties," *William and Mary Quarterly*, 3d ser., 32 (January 1975): 30, 49 (including note 55).

13. Viewed from a different angle of vision, as North Carolina matured economically, wealth increasingly became concentrated in the hands of an upper class, the composition of which essentially remained stable. In short, the heirs of this class inherited and built upon their parents' legacies, and slaves consequently became more and more concentrated in the hands of wealthy owners. A computer-aided wealth and mobility analysis of North Carolina done by the present authors and Calman Winegarden demonstrates the inequitable distribution of wealth in the colony and how powerfully wealth predicted wealth from decade

to decade in mature economic areas of the province. See Marvin L. Michael Kay and Lorin Lee Cary, "Class, Mobility, and Conflict in North Carolina on the Eve of the Revolution," in Jeffrey J. Crow and Larry E. Tise, eds., *The Southern Experience in the American Revolution* (Chapel Hill: University of North Carolina Press, 1978), pp. 115–23. Also see Tables 3-1, 3-2, 3-3, and 3-5 in this essay.

14. See Table 3-5 and Allan Kulikoff, "The Origins of Afro-American Society in Tidewater Maryland and Virginia, 1700 to 1790," *William and Mary Quarterly*, 3d ser., 35 (April 1978): 246–49.

15. See Menard, "The Maryland Slave Population, 1658 to 1730," pp. 29–54; Allan Kulikoff, "The Beginnings of the Afro-American Family in Maryland," in Aubrey C. Land, Lois Green Carr, and Edward C. Papenfuse, eds., *Law, Society, and Politics in Early Maryland* (Baltimore: Johns Hopkins University Press, 1977), pp. 171–96.

16. See Allan Kulikoff, "A 'Prolifick' People: Black Population Growth in the Chesapeake Colonies, 1700–1790," *Southern Studies* 16 (Winter 1977): 398–99; Kulikoff, "Origins of Afro-American Society," p. 231.

17. Kulikoff intelligently and persuasively develops these demographic interrelationships in "Black Population Growth in the Chesapeake."

18. We analyze this in depth in our forthcoming book on slavery in North Carolina, 1748–72.

19. See the note on sources and methods to Table 3-7 for a discussion of how imbalance ratios were constructed.

20. See the notes to Tables 3-6 and 3-7 for citations of the sources used to construct the tables.

21. See the note on sources and methods to Table 3-6 for a discussion of how the above percentages were derived.

22. Herbert Gutman, *The Black Family in Slavery and Freedom, 1750–1925* (New York: Random House, 1976); Kulikoff, "Beginnings of the Afro-American Family in Maryland."

23. Kulikoff, "Black Population Growth in the Chesapeake," p. 403.

24. These questions will be examined in detail in our forthcoming book on slavery in North Carolina, 1748–72.

25. See Ira Berlin, *Slaves without Masters: The Free Negro in the Antebellum South* (New York: Pantheon, 1974), pp. 3–50, and his "The Revolution in Black Life," in Alfred F. Young, ed., *The American Revolution: Explorations in the History of American Radicalism* (DeKalb: Northern Illinois University Press, 1976), pp. 347–82; John Hope Franklin, *The Free Negro in North Carolina, 1790–1860* (1943; reprint ed., New York: Russell and Russell, 1969), pp. 7, 9–14.

26. Berlin, "The Revolution in Black Life," pp. 352–61, and his *Slaves without Masters*, pp. 46–47.

27. For excellent recent analyses of blacks in North Carolina during the era of the American Revolution see Crow, *The Black Experience in Revolutionary North Carolina*; Jeffrey J. Crow, "Slave Rebelliousness and Social Conflict in North Carolina, 1775 to 1802," *William and Mary Quarterly*, 3d ser., 37 (January 1980): 79–102. See Berlin, *Slaves without Masters*, pp. 47, 137, for the proportion of blacks who were free in North Carolina from 1790 to 1860. The proportion rose from 4.7 percent in 1790 to 8.5 percent in 1840, where it stabilized until the Civil War.

28. See especially Berlin, *Slaves without Masters*, pp. 6–7; Berlin, "The Revolution in Black Life," pp. 352–53.

29. Notes to Tables 3-1, 3-5, and 3-6 contain sources for this statement.

30. Walter Clark, ed., *The State Records of North Carolina*, 16 vols., numbered 11–26 (Winston and Goldsboro: State of North Carolina, 1895–1906), 23:106–7.

31. See notes to Table 3-12.

32. For the laws in question see Clark, ed., *State Records*, 23:65, 195. See notes to Table 3-12 for the court orders summarized in the text.

33. See n. 32.

34. See Clark, ed., *State Records*, 23:195, and notes to Table 3-12.

35. See notes to Table 3-12; Berlin, *Slaves without Masters*, p. 6; Berlin, "The Revolution in Black Life," p. 352. See also James Blackwell Browning, "The Free Negro in Antebellum North Carolina," *North Carolina Historical Review* 15 (January 1938): 23.

36. See notes to Table 3-8.

37. Craven County Court Minutes, 1750–72; Edgecombe County Court Minutes, 1757–72; Orange County Court Minutes, 1752–66; Beaufort County—Minutes, Appearances, Prosecution, and Trial Docket, Court of Pleas and Quarter Sessions, vol. 1, 1756–61; Chowan County Court Minutes, 1748–72; New Hanover County Court Minutes, 1748–69, 1771–72, North Carolina State Archives.

38. Herbert Gutman develops a similar analysis concerning the effects of sale and whipping upon numerous slaves in addition to those actually sold or whipped. For instance, see his *Slavery and the Numbers Game: A Critique of "Time on the Cross"* (Urbana: University of Illinois Press, 1975), especially pp. 18–20, 126–31.

39. For documentation see sources listed in notes to Table 3-12.

4. The Black Female American Missionary Association Teacher in the South, 1861–1870

Linda M. Perkins

The efforts of the northern black female in the education of her race in the South during and after the Civil War have frequently been overlooked in educational history. Motivated primarily by the philosophy of self-help and race solidarity espoused within the black communities of the North, hundreds of black women journeyed south after the outbreak of war in 1861. This philosophy of "race uplift" was a compelling force in the lives of pre–Civil War blacks. Because black men and women were relegated to the lowest strata of American society, the efforts of members of both groups were necessary for the "elevation" of the race.

Although blacks also taught through the sponsorship of various private benevolent organizations and the federally funded Freedmen's Bureau, this discussion will be limited to the efforts of black women within the American Missionary Association (AMA) from 1861 to 1870. During this period, several thousand New England and northern women migrated to the South to teach the newly freed slaves. Most studies that examine these efforts overlook the small number of black women who were part of this educational crusade. An examination of black women's activities within the AMA provides greater insight into the educational philosophy of "race uplift" held by blacks, regardless of gender. In addition, as will be discussed, despite their common gender black and white women teachers differed in their desires and motivations and in the experiences they encountered.

Established in 1846 by a group of Congregationalist abolitionists, the AMA was a pioneer in the education of blacks. The association was the first and largest benevolent group to establish

Fig. 4-1. Northern white females under the auspices of the American Missionary Association traveled south to teach emancipated slaves after the Civil War. Northern black females also sought affiliation with the AMA in the work of educating their race. From J. T. Trowbridge, *The South: A Tour of Its Battle Fields and Ruined Cities; a Journey through the Desolated States, and Talks with the People* (Hartford, Conn.: L. Stubbins, 1866), facing p. 338.

formal educational institutions in the South for blacks, and it has been the focus of numerous studies.[1] The lack of knowledge about the activities, observations, and motivations of blacks within the AMA, however, has resulted in a skewed and unbalanced perspective on the group's educational efforts on behalf of blacks.[2]

The great majority of women who answered the call to go south under the auspices of the AMA were white, from New England or other parts of the North, and upper or middle class. The contributions of these women are well known. While traditional studies consistently cite altruism and abolitionist zeal as the forces that impelled these women to undertake this activity, a close examination of their letters, testimonies, and reports suggests a different interpretation.

Upper- and middle-class New England white women were constrained by the Victorian concept of "true womanhood." These women were educated for their "proper sphere"—to become wives and mothers—and not expected to work except in the event of financial necessity. Consequently, many young, well-educated New England women saw teaching in the South primarily as an escape from their idle and unfulfilled lives.[3]

The letters of application from white females to the AMA national office in New York often reflected the need to obtain refuge from the entrapment of New England life. One writer, in what was a common theme, stated, "My circumstances are such that it is necessary for me to be doing something." Frequently, fathers would write the AMA requesting employment for their daughters. One such father declared that his family was financially comfortable and that his daughter had completed high school and three years at Mt. Holyoke Seminary. She had traveled in Europe, was twenty-seven years old, and was living at home. The daughter had never worked because there was no reason for her to do so; however, she wished to go south "to do more good than she thinks she is doing at home." Many widows also applied. One applicant was brief and to the point: "I am a soldier's widow—left alone. I desire to be busy—useful."[4]

In a study of female teachers of the AMA who served in Georgia from 1865 to 1873, Jacqueline Jones concurs with the above thesis and also finds white females "joined the cause in order to liberate themselves from the comfort and complacency of a middle-class existence. . . . The work fulfilled some of their needs and enabled them to understand their own situation more clearly."[5]

Many of the letters of application from New England women no doubt came from the AMA's active recruitment efforts. Capitalizing upon the Victorian socialization of women to be self-sacrificing and dutiful, the AMA issued a pamphlet entitled *Woman's Work for the Lowly*. The publication urged females to fulfill their proper sphere, rather than remain "merely ornaments in their fathers' parlors, dreaming, restless, hoping, till some fortunate mating shall give them a home and a sphere."[6] Because of the eagerness of many women to go south, it was economical for the AMA to employ them. Not only were women paid less than men, but on occasion the women paid their own travel south and donated their entire salaries to the organization.[7] Few, however, envisioned their adventure south as anything other than a temporary one. Between 1860 and 1870 the average tenure of the white female educator was two to three years.[8]

As women of the larger society sought ways to improve the quality of their lives during the mid-nineteenth century, free black men and women struggled together to obtain freedom for their enslaved race. By the Civil War the shared experience of racial oppression had imbued these blacks with a deep sense of responsibility for members of their race. Thus, when war commenced in 1861, black men and women eagerly volunteered their services in the Union army.[9]

Many exiled southern black women living in the North returned to their homeland. For example, the legendary Harriet Tubman offered her services as a spy, nurse, and scout for the Union army. Mary Shadd Cary, who migrated to Canada in the 1850s, rushed back to the States after the outbreak of the war to serve as a scout for the Union army. And Louise De Mortie, a noted lecturer who had migrated from Virginia to Boston in the 1850s, moved to New Orleans in 1865 to open that city's first orphanage for black youth.[10]

Black women of the South also contributed greatly in the "uplift" of their race. Mary S. Peake, a prosperous woman from Hampton, Virginia, was found teaching in Fortress Monroe when the first AMA missionary, Lewis C. Lockwood, arrived to establish a school in September 1861. The association designated Peake's school its first institution in the South.[11]

The AMA soon established other schools in Virginia for the thousands of abandoned slaves. Although from the beginning the association employed black monitors within the schools, by 1863 officials had begun to seek black teachers. Missionaries had observed that blacks had more influence over the freed slaves than whites. On this point William Woodbury, AMA superintendent of schools, wrote George Whipple, AMA secretary, "It is a fact, that with the requisite culture, the colored teachers will get nearer to their own race in a thousand and one ways, than can the same grade of white talent."[12]

Woodbury's reference to "culture" reflected the AMA's belief in the superiority of New England culture. More than any other benevolent association the AMA sought teachers of New England and northern education, "culture and refinement." These qualifications, of course, limited the number of black women who sought employment with the AMA in the Civil War years. While certain normal schools admitted an occasional black woman, Oberlin College in Ohio was the only institution that admitted them on a regular basis.

Yet from this small number of educated black women of the North letters of application were received in the AMA's national office. According to their applications, these women, like most women of their race, were employed and financially supporting family members. The presence of dependent children normally prevented otherwise qualified black women from receiving positions with the AMA. For example, Lucie Stanton Day, the first black woman to complete the Ladies Department at Oberlin College (1850), was rejected by the association for a teaching post because she supported a seven-year-old daughter. Likewise, a widow, Mary S. Leary of Oberlin, was also refused by the AMA because she had a child. While these conditions disqualified black women for AMA employment, they did not necessarily exclude white women. White females with children frequently received appointments as matrons of AMA mission houses.[13]

The double standard utilized in the selection of black and white AMA employees reinforced Afro-American suspicions about the prejudice of abolitionists. Because the black women were not financial assets to the AMA and were burdened with having to demonstrate their "culture and refinement," their applications received greater scrutiny from the organization. From the outset the AMA viewed the black female applications with caution and regarded the initial black educators as "experiments."

The meager AMA salary of fifteen dollars per month seemingly would have deterred poor black women from applying. The deep conviction of duty to race frequently mentioned in the women's applications, however, overshadowed possible monetary gain as a motivation. The statement of one black woman applicant who characterized herself as "possessing no wealth and having nothing to give but my life to my work" reflected the level of poverty and depth of commitment of most of the women.[14]

The theme of "race uplift" characterized the letters of the women. A black woman from Rhode Island wrote, "Sir, I have a great desire to go and labor among the Freedmen of the South. I think it is our duty as a people to spend our lives in trying to elevate our own race. Who can feel for us if we do not feel for ourselves? And who can feel the sympathy that we can who are identified with them?" Lucie Stanton Day of Ohio also noted, "My sense of duty urge me to write. . . . I wish to engage in this work because I desire the elevation of my race." And Sara G. Stanley of Ohio, but originally from New Bern, North Carolina, reiterated "duty" as the motivation in applying for a teaching post. She wrote, "I have felt a strong conviction of duty. . . . I am bound to that ignorant, degraded, long enslaved race, by the ties of love and consanguinity; they are . . . my people."[15]

The black women emphatically expressed the belief that blacks should aid in the massive educational efforts of the South. Further, because of the kinship of northern blacks to the freed blacks, the women believed they were better equipped to serve their people than whites. Although AMA officials also recognized the tremendous influence of black teachers upon the freedmen, they viewed the black teachers primarily as cultural role models and not as potential authority figures within the organization.

Five black women were selected to go to Virginia in 1863 and 1864. Three of the women were from Oberlin College: Blanche Harris, a native of Michigan; Clara Duncan of Pittsfield, Massachusetts; and Sara G. Stanley. The other two were Sallie Daffin, a native of Philadelphia and a graduate of the Institute for Colored Youth of that city, and Edmonia G. Highgate of Syracuse, New York, a graduate of a normal school of her state.[16]

In a study of the AMA, Clara DeBoer states that the organization was "color-blind" in its treatment of black employees. The treatment of these five black women, however, contradicts that statement. Upon their arrival in Norfolk they quickly encountered conditions quite unlike those of their white colleagues. First, they were housed separately from the white teachers. Then when it was discovered that the school held in the Methodist church was to have an all-black staff, the trustees quickly moved the classes to the small, unventilated basement of the building.[17]

The all-black school staff was successful, nonetheless, until the illness of Harris and the transfer of several of the black women teachers ended the "experiment" after only several months. Although the women remained in the area and taught in other localities, their original school continued with an interracial staff.[18]

By the summer of 1864 the women had moved into the mission house with the other white teachers. No open arms greeted them there. Throughout the summer the women sent letters complaining about their treatment to Superintendent Woodbury, who had returned north. Stanley and Highgate reported that the white teachers commented constantly on the alleged inferiority of blacks and observed sharp social distinctions toward blacks. Daffin and Duncan wrote that the white matron of the mission house had "no interest in the cause" and requested her dismissal.[19]

By fall conditions had worsened. Another mission house director, a Miss Gleason, objected to having black teachers board at the house. This indignity prompted Stanley to write two letters regarding "prejudice against complexion." Stanley pointedly wrote AMA Secretary Whipple that she refused to move and was "much pained" that the association would place in such a position of authority a person who was "a very serious obstacle in the way of the advancement of the work." Moreover, in Stanley's estimation the woman lacked "thorough" intellectual training compared to many of the other teachers. Despite Stanley's letters Gleason remained in her position.[20]

The expectations of the black teachers and of the AMA regarding those who educated the freed blacks differed widely. The women expected competent, race-sensitive, and dedicated whites to be affiliated with the AMA. Never neglecting an opportunity to speak on behalf of the former slaves, Stanley wrote the national office in 1864 expressing her opinions about the teaching staff. She explained in her letter that racist and insensitive teachers would have "delerious effects [*sic*]" upon the black community. Although not visibly black, Stanley strongly identified with her race and suffered all the distinctions that racism placed on blacks. Explaining that she mingled constantly and freely with the blacks of all classes and knew their feelings, Stanley wrote, "My motive is to utter a plea for those who have no voice to plead for themselves." In closing she candidly declared that blacks preferred black teachers and recognized their true friends not through "*word* but *deed*."[21]

Recent research in black educational history suggests that a large majority of blacks preferred black teachers for their children during the nineteenth century. This conviction resulted not from ethnic chauvinism, as some have argued, but rather from a situation Stanley identified—racist teachers had a deleterious effect upon black pupils.[22] In addition, black parents doubtless understood the importance of a former slave child's having a black person as an authority figure.

Despite the letters to the national office the racial climate did not improve. By the spring of 1865 all of the black teachers who had arrived in Norfolk in 1864 had relocated to other parts of the country. There the women discovered that the racism they had experienced in Virginia was not an aberration but the norm with the AMA. For example, Blanche Harris and her sister were assigned posts in Natchez, Mississippi, in 1865. She reported in her first letter to the national office of the AMA the "marked" distinctions made between the black and white teachers by the local AMA. The Harris sisters were not assigned schools, were housed with the servants of the AMA, and received repeated insults. Even though the women refused to leave Mississippi, Harris admitted she and her sister often thought of resigning. When they remembered the work to be done, however, they were "willing to sacrifice much to see [their] race elevated."[23]

Edmonia Highgate was far less tolerant of discrimination and rarely apologized when she criticized the AMA. Prior to the Civil War she served as an agent for the National Freedmen Relief Association of New York City. When she applied to the AMA in 1863 at the age of twenty, she had taught two and a half years and was principal of one of the public schools for blacks in Binghamton, New York. For Highgate to go south required her relinquishing a position of prestige and money. In her initial letter of application to the AMA, Highgate stressed her commitment to blacks in the South and stated she was resigning a job that paid twice as much as the one offered by the AMA.[24]

In March 1865, Highgate was assigned to teach in Darlington,

Maryland. From the day of her arrival she was disappointed in the position and immediately informed the AMA of her intention to resign as soon as she organized a school and found a replacement. Because the area had only two hundred black residents, Highgate had to make laborious climbs over difficult terrain to reach only a handful of pupils. She often articulated the belief to the AMA that first-rate black teachers should receive maximum exposure among blacks. Highgate frankly informed the AMA officials that with her qualifications she should be in the "front ranks" as a "first teacher." Why, she asked, should she stay in the woods teaching thirty-four pupils when she could be reaching hundreds? Less than two months later she left to accept a post in Richmond, Virginia, with the Freedmen's Bureau.[25] Not committed to any benevolent organization but only to the "uplift" of her race, Highgate taught in Louisiana and Mississippi during the 1860s through the sponsorship of several organizations. In these locations Highgate narrowly escaped death by yellow fever and was shot at twice in her Mississippi school.[26]

The AMA began to focus on normal and collegiate training once its elementary schools were absorbed into the public school system after 1870. At this time Highgate wrote AMA officials of her decision to spend the rest of her days as a teacher at the recently established AMA normal school at Tougaloo, Mississippi (1869). Confidently informing the men of her qualifications, Highgate cited her experiences and noted her certificate of normal training from the Syracuse Board of Education. She remarked, "Only caste prevents me from occupying" a teaching position in Syracuse.[27] Unfortunately, the decision to teach at Tougaloo was not entirely in the hands of Highgate. With the AMA, as with the Syracuse Board of Education, caste would prevent her from obtaining the post. Even by 1895 of the 110 faculty members at the five AMA colleges, only 4 were black. And at the seventeen AMA secondary schools at this time, only 12 of the 141 teachers were black.[28]

Although DeBoer has asserted that "efficiency and economy rather than race dictated the placement of the AMA teachers," the experiences of Highgate and the other black women refute this statement.[29] It was a common practice of the association to send blacks to the most undesirable locations, assign them to teach only primary grades, and place them in small schools. Even though 105 of the 533 employees commissioned by the AMA before 1870 were black, most were student or assistant teachers and ministers. Because of the low positions of the black AMA employees and the stringent requirements of the association that blacks had to meet in order to become regular teachers, only 34 of the 105 were from the North.[30]

The desire of the AMA to dominate black education frequently sabotaged black efforts. Jacqueline Jones found in Georgia that the AMA not only had great contempt for independent black teachers but was also "perverse in [its] attempt to thwart efforts at black self-help in education." Jones's research further suggests that the association attempted to limit the influence of black teachers on black students by frequently denying teaching commissions to literate blacks.[31]

Revisionist historians have concluded that New England ethnocentrism and the refusal of the AMA administration to employ blacks in prominent positions had a negative impact upon the education of blacks. On this point historian Carter G. Woodson observed in 1933 that the missionary educators sought to "transform and not develop" blacks. In a study of student rebellions on black college campuses in the 1920s, Raymond Wolters has traced the source of the students' protests to the condescension of the nineteenth-century missionary educators.[32]

Although traditional studies in educational history have often indicated that blacks welcomed the missionary efforts with "open arms," evidence suggests that this belief is greatly overstated. Frederick Douglass, a critic of benevolent societies, expressed his apprehensions regarding such groups in 1865, when he observed that these groups tended to give blacks pity and not justice. In 1865 the *Christian Recorder*, the organ of the African Methodist Episcopal church, did not let the disparity between the principles and practices of some missionaries go unremarked. In an editorial the paper condemned those missionaries "who, while in the North make loud pretension to Abolition, when they get South partake so largely of that contemptible prejudice that they are ashamed to be seen in company with colored men."[33]

The efforts of the black teacher in the South during and after the Civil War demand further examination. Oppressed themselves by racism but genuinely committed to assisting the advancement of their race, northern black females possessed different motivations from and endured experiences in sharp contrast to those of white educators. Few of the black women saw their task as a temporary one. In a letter to the AMA, Clara Duncan wrote that in spite of hardships, "I am prepared to give up everything even life for the good of the cause, and count it not a hardship but an honor and blessing to me." Similarly, Sallie Daffin received numerous offers of higher salaries and better facilities for teaching posts in and near her home of Philadelphia, but wrote the AMA that she could never teach in the North again after realizing the needs of her race in the South. Edmonia Highgate relinquished a comfortable position in the North and pledged her life to work in the South. Braving, among other things, bullets and yellow fever, Highgate wrote, "I must do or die for my freed brethren." And Blanche Harris's statement from Mississippi that she had to "suffer many things" to see her race elevated expressed the attitude of the many black women who decided to devote their lives to the "cause."[34]

While current scholarship is reviewing more closely the dynamics of intraracial class, color, and cultural differences, the earliest black female teachers insisted that they did not see themselves as distinct from the freed blacks. One such black New England female teacher of a Freedmen's Bureau school in Mississippi wrote in 1866: "I class myself with the freedmen. . . . Though I have never known servitude they are . . . my people. Born as far north as the lakes, I have never felt no freer because so many were less fortunate."[35]

It is probable that the black women educators saw little difference between themselves and their southern kin, for in reality they were not treated differently. In spite of their light skin and privileged education the women were not strangers to racism. When on her voyage to her post in Virginia in 1864 it was discovered that Clara Duncan was black, she was refused meal service, was referred to as a "nigger wench," and was forced to ride in a separate compartment. All of the women had similar experiences.[36] Even within the AMA black women were often treated as servants.

Consequently, these women understood that the typical criterion for their treatment was normally color and not class or culture.

Despite the many acts of discrimination toward blacks by the AMA, the women sometimes found within the organization persons of goodwill and genuine friendship. Several of the white female teachers wrote letters of protest to the New York office when they observed that the black female teachers were housed in a separate residence in Norfolk in 1864. Martha L. Kellogg, a white teacher in Wilmington, North Carolina, wrote the AMA of her indignation at the treatment of black teachers and asked to be transferred.[37]

Except for the white females who taught in the AMA normal schools and colleges in the South, most whites returned north after 1870. For the black female teacher, however, the mission of "uplifting" her race remained an important and unfinished task. Barred from employment within the AMA schools, black women became the backbone of the public schools for blacks in the South by the end of the century.

Remembering these efforts, black scholar W. E. B. Du Bois wrote in 1920, "After the [Civil] War the sacrifice of Negro women for freedom and uplift is one of the finest chapters in their history."[38] The black women AMA teachers were an important force in this history.

NOTES

1. Literature on the subject includes: Richard B. Drake, "The American Missionary Association and the Southern Negro, 1861–88," Ph.D. diss., Emory University, 1957; Elizabeth Jacoway, *Yankee Missionaries in the South: The Penn School Experiment* (Baton Rouge: Louisiana State University Press, 1980); Clifton Herman Johnson, "The American Missionary Association, 1841–61: A Study of Christian Abolitionism," Ph.D. diss., University of North Carolina, 1958; Jacqueline Jones, *Soldiers of Light and Love: Northern Teachers and Georgia Blacks, 1865–73* (Chapel Hill: University of North Carolina Press, 1980); James M. McPherson, *The Abolitionist Legacy: From Reconstruction to the NAACP* (Princeton: Princeton University Press, 1975); James M. McPherson, *The Struggle for Equality: Abolitionists and the Negro in*

the Civil War and Reconstruction (Princeton: Princeton University Press, 1964); Willie Lee Rose, *Rehearsal for Reconstruction: The Port Royal Experiment* (New York: Oxford University Press, 1964); Henry Lee Swint, *The Northern Teacher in the South, 1862–70* (New York: Octagon Books, 1941); Elizabeth Botume, *First Days amongst the Contrabands* (Boston: Lee and Shepard, 1893); Laura M. Towne, *Letters and Diary of Laura M. Towne, Written from the Sea Islands of South Carolina, 1862–84*, edited by Rupert Sargent Holland (Cambridge: Printed at Riverside Press, 1912).

2. Men represented a large percentage of black AMA employees by Reconstruction. Most, however, were from the South, as were the women by this time. For statistics on black AMA teachers see Clara Merritt DeBoer, "The Role of Afro-Americans in the Origin and Work of the American Missionary Association, 1839–77," Ph.D. diss., Rutgers University, 1973, p. 492.

3. For a discussion of "true womanhood" see Barbara Welter, "The Cult of True Womanhood, 1820–60," *American Quarterly* 18 (Summer 1966): 151–74. Similar reasons accounted for the proliferation of women in the abolitionist movement. See Barbara Berg, *The Remembered Gate: Origins of American Feminism, the Woman, and the City, 1800–1860* (New York: Oxford University Press, 1978), p. 161.

4. Jones, *Soldiers of Light and Love*, p. 42.

5. Ibid., p. 8; Kate Mattison, Mt. Vernon, Ohio, to Reverend S. S. Jocelyn, March 1864, in American Missionary Association Papers, Amistad Research Center, Dillard University, New Orleans, La.

6. As quoted in McPherson, *Abolitionist Legacy*, p. 165.

7. Jones, *Soldiers of Light and Love*, p. 37.

8. McPherson, *Abolitionist Legacy*, p. 165.

9. James M. McPherson, *The Negro's Civil War: How American Negroes Felt and Acted during the War for the Union* (New York: Vintage Books, 1965), pp. 173–244; Susan King Taylor, *Reminiscences of My Life in Camp* (1902; reprint ed., New York: Arno Press, 1969).

10. Sarah Bradford, *Harriet Tubman: The Moses of Her People* (Secaucus, N.J.: Citadel Press, 1974), pp. 31–32; biographical folder and Martin Delany to Mary Shadd Cary, 7 December 1853, Mary Shadd Cary Papers, Moorland-Spingarn Research Center, Howard University; John W. Blassingame, *Black New Orleans, 1860–80* (Chicago: University of Chicago Press, 1973), p. 170; George Washington Williams, *A History of the Negro Race in America*, 2 vols. (New York: Bergman Publishers, 1883), 2:449.

11. Lewis C. Lockwood, *Mary S. Peake: The Colored Teacher at*

Fortress Monroe (Boston: American Tract Society, 1863), pp. 5, 14; Lewis C. Lockwood, Fortress Monroe, to AMA Executive Committee, 24 February 1862, AMA Papers.

12. William H. Woodbury, Norfolk, Virginia, to George Whipple, 7 November 1863, AMA Papers.

13. Lucie Stanton Day, Cleveland, Ohio, to George Whipple, 26 April 1864; Mary S. Leary, Oberlin, Ohio, to George Whipple, 17 September 1867, AMA Papers. During the period that Day sought a position with the AMA the organization employed a white female with four children to serve as matron of the mission house in Norfolk. See Clara C. Duncan, Norfolk, to William Woodbury, 29 August 1864, AMA Papers. The author wishes to thank Ellen Henle for directing her to the references on Day and Leary.

14. Sara G. Stanley, Cleveland, Ohio, to George Whipple, 19 January 1864, AMA Papers.

15. Mrs. E. Garrison Jackson, Newport, Rhode Island, to S. S. Jocelyn, 13 June 1864; Lucie Stanton Day, Cleveland, Ohio, to George Whipple, 26 April 1864; Sara S. Stanley, Cleveland, Ohio, to George Whipple, 19 January and 4 March 1864, AMA Papers.

16. Ellen Henle and Marlene Merrill, "Antebellum Black Coeds at Oberlin College," *Women's Studies Newsletter* 7 (Spring 1979): 10. Mrs. M. P. Dascomb, Oberlin, Ohio, to George Whipple, 2 March 1864; Edmonia Highgate to the Reverend E. P. Smith, 23 July 1870, AMA Papers. Fanny Jackson Coppin, *Reminiscences of School Life and Hints on Teaching* (Philadelphia: AME Book Concern, 1913), pp. 147, 184.

17. DeBoer, "The Role of Afro-Americans," p. viii.

18. Edmonia G. Highgate, Portsmouth, Virginia, to George Whipple, 30 April 1864; Sara S. Smith, Norfolk, to George Whipple, 15 March 1864, AMA Papers.

19. Sara G. Stanley and Edmonia Highgate, Norfolk, to William Woodbury, 21 July 1864; Sallie Daffin, Norfolk, to William Woodbury, 29 August 1864; Clara Duncan, Norfolk, to William Woodbury, 29 August 1864, AMA Papers.

20. Sara G. Stanley, Norfolk, to George Whipple, 6 October 1864, AMA Papers.

21. Sara G. Stanley, Norfolk, to William Woodbury, 21 July 1864, AMA Papers.

22. Carlton Mabee, *Black Education in New York State* (Syracuse: Syracuse University Press, 1979), p. 97; see also chapter 15, "The Struggle for Black Control," in McPherson, *Abolitionist Legacy*.

23. Blanche Harris, Natchez, Mississippi, to George Whipple, 23 January and 10 March 1866, AMA Papers.

24. Edmonia Highgate, Binghamton, New York, to George Whipple, 18 and 30 January, 17 February 1864, AMA Papers.

25. Edmonia Highgate, Darlington, Maryland, to George Whipple, 13 April 1865, AMA Papers.

26. Edmonia Highgate, Lafayette Parish, to Michael E. Strieby, 8 February 1866, and same, New Orleans, to Strieby, 24 September 1867, AMA Papers.

27. Edmonia Highgate, Cortland, New York, to the Reverend E. P. Smith, 23 July 1870, AMA Papers.

28. McPherson, *Abolitionist Legacy*, p. 273.

29. DeBoer, "The Role of Afro-Americans," p. 493.

30. Ibid., p. 326.

31. Jones, *Soldiers of Light and Love*, p. 206.

32. Raymond Wolters, *The New Negro on Campus* (Princeton: Princeton University Press, 1975), pp. 340–41; Carter G. Woodson, *Mis-education of the Negro* (Washington, D.C.: Associated Publishers, Inc., 1933), p. 17.

33. See Joel Williamson, "Black Self-Assertion before and after Emancipation," in Nathan I. Huggins, Martin Kilson, Daniel M. Fox, eds., *Key Issues in the Afro-American Experience* (New York: Harcourt, Brace Jovanovich, 1971), p. 225; *Christian Recorder*, 2 December 1865, as quoted in McPherson, *The Struggle for Equality*, p. 397.

34. Clara C. Duncan, Norfolk, to William Woodbury, 29 August 1864; Sallie Daffin, Norfolk, to George Whipple, 20 February 1865; Edmonia G. Highgate, New York, to Michael E. Strieby, 26 October 1864; Blanche Harris, Natchez, Mississippi, to George Whipple, 10 March 1866, AMA Papers.

35. As quoted in Leon F. Litwack, *Been in the Storm So Long: The Aftermath of Slavery* (New York: Knopf, 1979), p. 512.

36. Marie Bassette, Norfolk, to George Whipple and S. S. Jocelyn, 24 March 1864; Samuel H. Walker, Norfolk, to Whipple, 28 March 1864; Clara C. Duncan, Norfolk, to George Whipple, 30 March 1864, AMA Papers.

37. DeBoer, "The Role of Afro-Americans," p. 278; Martha L. Kellogg, Wilmington, North Carolina, to AMA, 5 November 1866, AMA Papers.

38. W. E. B. Du Bois, *Darkwater: Voices from within the Veil* (New York: Schocken Books, 1969), p. 178.

5. A Comparative Perspective on Race Relations in Southern and Northern Cities, 1860–1900, with Special Emphasis on Raleigh

Howard N. Rabinowitz

This essay attempts to do three things. First, and most important, it attempts to outline in very general terms the basic developments in southern urban race relations between 1860 and 1900. Second, it tries to show how the black experience in Raleigh reflected these broader trends. Finally, it suggests some possible similarities and differences between the experiences of blacks in northern and southern cities during the period.[1]

Like the rest of American cities in the latter part of the nine-teenth century, southern cities grew in population largely as a result of migration. Elsewhere in the country the migrants were either foreigners or rural whites; in the South large numbers of rural whites moved to the cities, but a more significant group was rural blacks. Like the Eastern Europeans in the North, the Chinese in the Far West, and the former farmers in the Midwest, these new urban dwellers in the South were a source of instability and social disruption. But blacks presented southern white urbanites with an even more serious problem. Not only were these newcomers poor, unaccustomed to the conditions and responsibilities of urban life, and of a different ethnic and racial background than a majority of the resident population, but they were also tainted by slavery. Unlike other migrants, blacks had long been assigned a role in the life of the region in which they settled. Their position had been one of subservience, as slaves controlled by the white race. A free

Negro was an anomaly, someone whom Southerners had sought to banish from their midst. North Carolina, for example, was among several states that considered formally expelling free Negroes, though in the end only Arkansas actually did so.[2] Now as a result of the Civil War all blacks were free.

By 1900, although only 17 percent of southern blacks lived in cities, they made up 31 percent of the region's urban population and 68 percent of the nation's Negro urban dwellers. Blacks were an even greater factor in North Carolina cities: 12.2 percent of the black population was urban, but blacks constituted 40.8 percent of all urban dwellers.[3] Better educated and more prosperous than their rural brothers, southern urban blacks played a major role in national Negro political, economic, and social affairs. Nevertheless, their imprint on urban society and the impact that city life had on them remain largely undocumented.

Urban historians, for example, have long slighted the South and have preferred to concentrate on a few large eastern and midwestern cities. Preoccupied with national policymaking and statewide trends, historians of the Reconstruction period have noted the urban scene only in passing. Students of black history have also tended to ignore the fate of these new migrants to southern towns and have viewed emancipation, as well as slavery, primarily within a rural context. Those interested in detailed descriptions of life in the postbellum years must turn to the growing number of monographs about black communities in the urban North, with a few recent exceptions.[4] As a result of these studies, it is commonly agreed that it was in the North during the twentieth century that the modern Negro ghetto first appeared. Yet the experience of blacks in late-nineteenth-century southern cities suggests a different conclusion.

Any attempt to understand postbellum race relations in the urban South must begin by considering the tremendous increase in the number of black urban dwellers between 1860 and 1870, even though the great majority of blacks remained in the countryside. The antebellum trend toward the thinning out of black urban populations was reversed, and the pattern of absolute and often relative increases in the black urban population so common until 1900 was established. Between 1860 and 1870 Atlanta's black popula-

Table 5-1. *Raleigh Population, 1850–1900*

	1850	1860	1870	1880	1890	1900
White	2,253	2,693	3,696	4,911	6,327	7,922
Black	2,263	2,087	4,094	4,354	6,348	5,721
Percentage Black	50.1	44	53	47	50.1	41.9

Source: U.S. Censuses, 1850–1900.

tion, for example, grew from 1,939 to 9,929, and the black percentage of the population rose from 20 percent to 46 percent. Nashville's black population increased from 23 percent to 38 percent, New Orleans's from 14.3 percent to 26.4 percent, and Raleigh's from 44 percent to 53 percent. Because of the undercount of urban blacks in the 1870 census, the actual increases were greater still.

Rural blacks came to the cities for a variety of reasons. For some, the cities, which were headquarters for the federal forces, represented safety from the violence and intimidation of the countryside. Others came for the welfare and educational services provided by the army, the Freedmen's Bureau, and northern missionary societies. No doubt others were drawn by the attractions of city life and the simple desire to exercise their new freedom of movement. Whatever the motivation, most realized that in the antebellum period the cities had been better places for blacks than the rural areas.

The influx of blacks and the resultant problem of social control greatly troubled whites. In their view the Negroes "infested" the cities, "clogged" the streets, and threatened peace and prosperity. Writing in the fall of 1867, the editor of the Raleigh *Weekly Progress* complained:

> For nearly three years Raleigh has been to the great mobs of unbleached Americans in the western and contiguous counties of this state what Mecca is to the followers of Mohamet

. . . caravan after caravan swarmed into the state capital—
the immigrants being principally the idle and the desolate
thus overcrowding our beautiful city with a population ca-
pable of at times being made a dangerous instrument in the
hands of vicious men.[5]

To whites, God had ordained a rural existence for blacks, or as the
Montgomery Daily Ledger put it most bluntly, "The city was
intended for white people."[6] But while whites sought to reestab-
lish the control weakened by the defeat of the Confederacy and the
emancipation of the slaves, blacks sought to use the urban environment to fulfill their dreams of freedom. At times the interests
of the whites and blacks coincided; more often, however, they
were in conflict. Out of this interaction between whites and blacks
there had evolved by 1900 a new pattern of race relations that
contained elements of both continuity and change.

The economic status of blacks affected all other aspects of
black urban life. As early as February 1867 a Raleigh newspaper
noted that "quite a number of colored people this year are embark-
ing in business."[7] By 1900 in Raleigh and elsewhere there had
emerged a small group of successful black caterers, contractors,
undertakers, grocers, lawyers, and teachers. Some, like Raleigh
livery business owner John O. Kelly, even employed whites. But
the majority of blacks were mired in the lowest-paying jobs: the
men were primarily employed as unskilled laborers and servants
and the women (who made up a far larger segment of the Negro
work force than did women among whites) worked almost entirely
as domestics and washerwomen. It is true that most Negroes
lacked the necessary skills to get better-paying jobs, but many had
been artisans either in antebellum cities or on the plantations. The
fact that so few found work as cabinetmakers, machinists, or
plumbers was due to the opposition of local whites, especially
those in unions, from which blacks were often barred. Thus at the
turn of the century a Raleigh resident reported that "the black
artisan is losing here"; a key reason was that there were no Negroes in the local unions, and "it is doubtful they could get in."[8]

Many blacks who worked as servants, gardeners, and laun-
dresses for their former masters lived in the old slave quarters

Fig. 5-1. Berry O'Kelly (1860–1931) epitomized the emergence of the black middle class in postbellum Raleigh. O'Kelly, a merchant and educator in Method, a black community in west Raleigh, was appointed postmaster in 1890. In 1914 he consolidated three rural black schools in Wake County to form the Berry O'Kelly Training Center in Method. Photograph from the files of the North Carolina Division of Archives and History, Raleigh.

behind their employers' houses. But a combination of white hostility, economic constraints, and black desires increased segregation and soon altered the antebellum pattern of integrated neighborhoods. Community institutions, such as churches, schools, meeting halls, and, in some cases, businesses, were located in black areas, thus foreshadowing the appearance of the twentieth-century northern ghettoes. Blacks concentrated in such areas as Atlanta's Shermantown or Summer Hill, Richmond's Jackson

Fig. 5-2. The Berry O'Kelly Store and the Method Post Office. Photograph from the files of the North Carolina Division of Archives and History, Raleigh.

Ward, and Nashville's Black Bottom or Rocktown, which were located on the fringes of the still-compact cities near railroad tracks, industrial sites, and contaminated streams. By 1881 almost all of the 750 inhabitants of Oberlin, a mile northwest of Raleigh, were black. And by the end of the decade the predominantly Negro Second and Fourth wards in the southern part of the city contained Raleigh's two Negro grade schools, six of the nine black churches, the Institution for the Colored Blind and Deaf and Dumb, Shaw Institute, the Colored Masonic Hall, and most of the Negro hotels, boardinghouses, and businesses. The few whites in black neighborhoods throughout the South came primarily from three groups with limited mobility: laborers, widows, and grocers.

In an effort to discourage the urban migration whites initially sought to deny blacks municipal services. But thanks to the intervention of federal authorities and the governments established under congressional Reconstruction, the antebellum policy of exclusion of blacks from schools and welfare services was replaced by one of segregated access. For the first time in most cities

Fig. 5-3. James H. Young (1859–1921), military officer, political leader, and Raleigh newspaper editor, was one of the most influential black Republicans in North Carolina in the 1890s. He was twice elected to represent Wake County in the North Carolina General Assembly (1894 and 1896). From J. A. Whitted, *History of Negro Baptists in North Carolina* (Raleigh: Edwards and Broughton, 1908), facing p. 133.

blacks were admitted to poorhouses, insane asylums, hospitals, and public schools. In 1868 North Carolina blacks, for example, gained access to segregated quarters in the state institutions for the insane and the blind, deaf, and dumb located in the Raleigh area. City authorities, however, often dragged their feet when it came to educating blacks, as was the case in Raleigh, where northern missionary societies ran the Negro schools until the city incorporated them into a segregated system in 1877. Most blacks supported the shift from exclusion to segregation in the hope that segregated accommodations could be truly equal. Yet while the Redeemers accepted the Republican commitment to end exclusion, they pursued a policy of separate but unequal treatment of blacks. Calls by blacks for better services were usually rebuffed, though blacks did obtain black teachers for most of the black schools and gained admission to several facilities previously closed to them. In fact, Raleigh remained one of the few cities in the South in which racially mixed faculties could still be found in black schools as late as 1890.

The shift from exclusion to segregation was also evident in militia service, fire fighting, and a variety of public accommodations and public conveyances. Despite the Civil Rights Act of 1875 and Negro protests about its weak enforcement, de facto segregation quickly became the rule in steamships, railroads, hotels, restaurants, skating rinks, parks, and theaters. When Dan Castello's Grand Circus played Raleigh in 1866, accommodations for blacks were segregated, as was the case soon after in the city's Tucker Hall. A decade later James O'Hara, one of North Carolina's leading black politicians and soon to be congressman from the state's famous Second District, told a congressional committee: "I have gone to theatres in Raleigh frequently; and I have seen no exclusion on account of color. I suppose if a colored man should attempt to take a principle seat in a theatre in North Carolina he would have the same difficulty as in New York."[9]

Raleigh was also typical in that throughout the late nineteenth century racial intermingling was perhaps greatest in the parks. Pullen and Brookside parks remained open to blacks well into the twentieth century. Yet blacks visiting Brookside could not use the swimming pool, a fact representative of the internal segregation evident in parks elsewhere. When a new zoo opened in Atlanta's Grant Park in 1890, it contained eight cages occupying the center of the building and stretching from one end to the other. Aisles seven feet wide were railed off on each side of the row of cages, one for blacks, the other for whites, each with its own entrance and exit doors. (It is not known if the animals were told which way to face.) After 1890 this type of segregation was buttressed by laws, and whatever limited flexibility there had been in places such as streetcars soon disappeared.

Segregation also dominated the religious life of southern cities, though this was more an example of continuity rather than change. At the end of the war blacks, among them the members of Raleigh's First Baptist, left segregated white congregations and formed their own churches (by 1885 four black churches had sprung from the Colored First Baptist, although nine hundred to a thousand of the city's fifteen hundred Negro Baptists still belonged to the mother church). Other black congregations that had been organized before the war, including Raleigh's St. Paul AME, joined these new bodies to help make Sunday the most segregated day of the week.

The church occupied the central position in the black community. Not simply a religious institution, it had recreational, economic, and political functions as well. Only in church affairs could blacks exercise a significant degree of independent control. (Even in church, however, blacks often called upon whites for financial or other kinds of assistance and went so far as to provide segregated seating during fund-raising meetings.) The Negro pastors, who quickly replaced whites, such as the presidents of St. Augustine's College and Shaw Institute, in most of the pulpits, acted as intermediaries between the black and white worlds of the city. Active in most areas of community life, they functioned mainly as a force for accommodation, but to a surprising degree, as in campaigns for better schools and black teachers, they also served as agents of protest. As the period waned, the old uneducated slave preachers were followed in the major pulpits by young college-trained pastors. For black congregants, their appearance, and the building of impressive new edifices, testified to the great progress of the race.

Fig. 5-4. First Baptist Church, which stands on Wilmington Street across from the State Capitol in Raleigh, was established about 1816. The present-day structure was built and the cornerstone laid in 1904 under the ministry of William Tyler Coleman. Date of photograph unknown. From the files of the North Carolina Division of Archives and History, Raleigh.

Fig. 5-5. William Tyler Coleman typified the new urban black ministers who, unlike the pastors they replaced, were college trained. Coleman, born in 1867 in Uniontown, Alabama, later earned an M.D. from Leonard Medical School at Shaw University in 1909. Photograph courtesy of First Baptist Church, Raleigh.

Fig. 5-6. St. Paul AME Church on Edenton Street in Raleigh was established in 1848 and rebuilt in 1884. After that church was destroyed by fire around the turn of the century, a new edifice was completed in 1910. Date of photograph unknown. From the files of the North Carolina Division of Archives and History, Raleigh.

In one area segregation was not enough. Despite white opposition blacks won the right to vote and hold office, the first time southern blacks had enjoyed political rights since the disfranchisement of Tennessee and North Carolina free Negroes in 1834 and 1835. Once this had been accomplished as a result of the Reconstruction acts, white Southerners sought, as in all other areas of southern life, to develop a system that would minimize the effect of the Negroes' freedom. Not until after 1890 did Southerners decide again on a path of wholesale de jure disfranchisement, and then only when they became convinced that Northerners would not interfere. In North Carolina disfranchisement did not come until 1900, when through a constitutional amendment, the passage of which was assured by a discriminatory 1899 election law, voters were subjected to a literacy test and required to pay a poll tax.[10]

In the interim, however, the idea of controlling the black vote was the central consideration in southern politics, especially on the local level. Therefore, the important question for the political experience of urban Negroes was not merely whether or not they could vote but what power did their votes have. The answer, not surprisingly, was that their ballots were most influential during Reconstruction. Blacks sat on the city councils of most southern cities and worked with varying degrees of success for the equal treatment of their race. Once the Redeemers consolidated their power through an artful combination of gerrymandering, vote fraud, actual and threatened retribution, and rigged voting laws, black political influence was removed or effectively isolated. Meanwhile, the Democrats made only half-hearted attempts to woo the blacks away from their traditional allegiance to the Republicans. The blacks largely resisted, but the Democrats did not really mind. Without their black component, the Republicans would have been less of a target; with sizable black support competing factions of Democrats would have faced the unpopular task of vying for black votes.

Raleigh's experience with black suffrage and officeholding was in many ways typical. Two of the nine-man city council appointed by Governor William Holden in 1868 were Negro, including James H. Harris, an upholsterer by trade but a politician by profession and the city's most prominent black leader. Once municipal elections began in 1869, blacks held approximately one-third of the seats until Republicans lost control of the city in 1875. And though biographical information is incomplete and often unreliable, it would seem that Raleigh's twenty-five Negro councilmen resembled their counterparts throughout the South.[11] As Table 5-2 indicates, all but one were native grown and all were literate. They came generally from the ranks of artisans and petty tradesmen, with the addition, especially toward the end of the century, of an occasional lawyer or teacher. According to the 1870 census, at least five of the thirteen for whom such information is available owned property worth at least one thousand dollars. Many were black and most probably former slaves, but there were disproportionate numbers of mulattoes and persons with free antecedents.[12] For the most part, these were relatively young men, in their thirties or early forties when first elected.

Yet Raleigh differed politically in significant ways from most other southern cities in the years between the end of Reconstruction and disfranchisement. Most important, blacks remained on the new expanded council until the turn of the century, rather than being excluded as was the norm elsewhere. As was true of North Carolina as a whole, Raleigh also witnessed less voter intimidation and fraud both during and after Reconstruction. And the strength and persistence of Republican influence in the city and state set Raleigh apart from all but a few cities in states other than North Carolina, Tennessee, and Virginia. Yet after Redemption the Democrats controlled the gerrymandered seventeen- and later twelve-man council, and except for the brief period of fusion rule by Populists and Republicans during the mid-1890s the three or four blacks usually elected had little of the political leverage they had enjoyed during Reconstruction. School appropriations became increasingly unequal, black policemen were removed, and the new city hospital excluded blacks. Finally, the last Negroes, James Hamlin and Charles Williams, left the council in May 1901, shortly after North Carolina's George H. White became the last southern black to serve in Congress until 1972.[13]

Such a broad overview does not do justice to the variety of the southern urban experience or to the changes in the status of blacks over time. We can, however, compare this general picture of race relations in the urban South with that of the North. The chief problem with such a comparison is not that meaningful distinctions between southern cities become blurred, but rather that the differences between northern cities prove so much greater than those between their southern counterparts.

In general the differences in patterns of race relations between northern and southern cities in this period are striking. Indeed, during no other period prior to the 1950s were these patterns in northern and southern cities more dissimilar than they were between 1860 and 1900. There were, of course, similarities, notably with regard to the central role in both sections of the Negro church and fraternal order. Yet even with these institutions there are differences, since in places like Cleveland, Detroit, and Boston and, to a lesser extent, in cities with larger black populations, members of the Negro elite could still be found in white churches, fraternal orders, and clubs.[14]

Differences are more evident in other areas. Most obviously, northern blacks were more heavily concentrated in cities, yet they constituted a small percentage of their region's urban population. In 1900, 70.5 percent of northern Negroes were urban, but they made up only 2.5 percent of the North's urban dwellers.[15] These demographic factors, and the presence of more whites committed to equal rights, greatly influenced northern urban race relations. At the same time that de jure segregation replaced de facto segregation in the South, for example, legal barriers between the races in the North came down. Whereas the Supreme Court decision in 1883 declaring the Civil Rights Act of 1875 unconstitutional added further support to existing discrimination in the South, it produced state legislation in the North that repealed antimiscegenation statutes and banned segregated schools and public accommodations. Segregation often persisted, but it was now in clear violation of the law.[16] Similarly, while first piecemeal and then de jure disfranchisement lessened the political power of southern blacks, the competition for Negro votes between two evenly matched political parties in the North brought northern blacks their greatest power during the 1880s and 1890s.[17]

Economic comparisons are more difficult. As in the South,

Table 5-2. *Raleigh Negro Councilmen, 1868–1901*

Name	Black Mulatto	Born	Birth-place	Died	Occupation in Office
James Baker	M (1870–80) B (1900)	1840	NC	NA[a]	grocer
John H. Brown	M	1850	NC	NA	carpenter
Reuben Cole	M	1844	NC	1927	grocer
M. Nelson Dunstan	B	1855	NC	NA	barber
Norfleet Dunstan	M (1870) B (1880)	1835	NC	1919	shoemaker
Stewart Ellison	B	c.1834	NC	NA	grocer, contractor
Albert Farrar	M (1860) B (1870)	1814	NC	NA	blacksmith
Bennett B. Goins	B	1854	NC	NA	teacher
James Hamlin	M	1859	Va.	1924	saloon-keeper, druggist
Andrew J. Harris	B?	1810?	NC	NA	porter
James H. Harris	M	c.1832	NC	1891	supt. inst. for colored deaf, dumb & blind
Charles W. Hoover	M	1853	NC	NA	huckster, bar owner

Property in 1870[b]	Council Service[c]	Literacy	Religion	Prewar Status[d]
$600 real $100 personal	1895–97 (1)	Yes	NA	NA
NA	1881–82 (1)	Yes	NA	NA
NA	1885–89 (2)	Yes	Baptist	NA
NA	1885–87 (1)	Yes	NA	NA
$700 real $300 personal	1869–72, 1877–83 (10)	Yes	NA	free
none listed	1869–76, 1877–79, 1880–84 (13)	Yes	NA	slave
$1,000 real	1869 (1)	Yes	NA	free
NA	1882–83 (1)	Yes	NA	NA
NA	1883–84, 1897–1901 (3)	Yes	Baptist (?)	NA
none listed	1887–89 (1)	Yes	NA	NA
$4,000 real $1,000 personal	1868, 1875–76, 1877–78, 1887–90 (4½)	Yes	Episcopal	free
NA	1879–85, 1895–97 (7)	Yes	NA	NA

Table 5-2. *(continued)*

Name	Black Mulatto	Born	Birth-place	Died	Occupation in Office
Americus Hunter	M	1845	NC	NA	box mail collector
Edward A. Johnson	M	1860	NC	1944	lawyer
Henry C. Jones	B (1870) M (1880)	c.1836	NC	NA	brickmason
James H. Jones	M	1832	NC	NA	bricklayer, tailor
Handy Lockhart	B	c.1795	NC	1884	undertaker, carpenter
W. H. Mathews	B	c.1828	NC	NA	brickmason
William Mitchell	M	1844	NC	1914	well digger brickmason
Virgil Ricks	M	c.1842	NC	NA	provision dealer
Nicholas F. Roberts	B	1849	NC	1934	college professor
B. J. Robinson	B	1860	NC	NA	grocer
Alfred Tate	M	1840	NC	NA	clerk
Charles Williams	B	1860	NC	NA	principal col. dept. deaf, dumb & blind ins
James H. Young	M	1859	NC	1921	clerk in revenue de

Property in 1870[b]	Council Service[c]	Literacy	Religion	Prewar Status[d]
none listed	1883–84 (1)	Yes	NA	NA
NA	1893–95, 1897–99 (2)	Yes	Congregation-alist	slave
none listed	1875–76 (1)	Yes	NA	NA
none listed	1873–76, 1877–89 (10)	Yes	NA	slave
$1,500 real $300 personal	1868 (1)	Yes	NA	NA
$1,100 real	1887–89 (1)	Yes	NA	NA
$325 real	1878–79 (1)	Yes	NA	free (?)
none listed	1873–74, 1879–80 (2)	Yes	Baptist(?)	NA
NA	1885–87 (1)	Yes	Baptist	NA
NA	1889–99 (5)	Yes	NA	NA
NA	1891–93 (1)	Yes	NA	NA
NA	1899—1901 (1)	Yes	Baptist(?)	NA
NA	1883–84 (1)	Yes	Baptist	NA

around 75 percent of northern urban black males were confined to the lowest-paying jobs. At least in some cities, however, their position improved or remained the same during the late nineteenth century, while conditions in the South deteriorated for those in similar circumstances. Northern female blacks certainly had more opportunities for advancement than their southern sisters. And the greater frequency of female-headed black families in the South further testifies to the stronger economic position of northern blacks.[18] Then, too, because of the relatively small number of blacks in most northern cities and the greater acceptance of integration, black businessmen and professionals could often rely on white clienteles, as their southern counterparts could not.[19] Although the matter is subject to debate, it would also appear that prior to 1900 residential segregation was less of a factor in northern than in southern cities, and members of the northern Negro elite had a far greater range of housing choices.[20]

The character of northern urban race relations would change after 1900 and especially after the so-called Great Migration.[21] Republican hegemony during the Fourth Party System (1894–1932) eliminated the incentive to woo northern Negro voters, and the growing number of black migrants (many of them from southern cities like Raleigh) alarmed whites at the same time that the massive influx of foreigners provided formidable competitors for blacks in the areas of housing and employment. But between 1860

Sources: U.S. Manuscript Census Schedules, 1860, 1870, 1880, 1900; Raleigh City Directories, 1866–1901; Miscellaneous Biographical Directories and Newspapers; North Carolina Board of Health, Deaths, 1906–29, North Carolina State Archives.

a. Not Available.

b. As listed in the 1870 census. Several men for whom none was listed certainly owned property as well.

c. Those appointed in 1868 served from 15 July to 5 January 1869; from then until 1885 elected terms were for one year, the elections in 1869 and 1870 coming in January and the remainder in May. Two-year terms were initiated in 1885 with elections in May. There were three wards with a total of nine councilmen between 1868 and 1874; five wards and seventeen councilmen from 1875 to 1893, and four wards with twelve councilmen for the remainder of the period. Figures in parentheses indicate the number of terms served.

d. See note 12.

and 1900, most notably after 1880, southern blacks who moved to northern cities usually enjoyed greater opportunities than those who remained behind. The last twenty years of the century witnessed a decline in the extent of legally enforced segregation and discrimination in the North, a greater role for blacks in politics, and perhaps an improvement in black prospects for economic success. After a more promising beginning, the social, political, and economic trends for blacks in the South ran in the opposite direction.

NOTES

1. Unless otherwise noted citations and supporting evidence can be found in the relevant chapters of Howard N. Rabinowitz, *Race Relations in the Urban South, 1865–1890* (New York: Oxford University Press, 1978).

2. Ira Berlin, *Slaves without Masters: The Free Negro in the Antebellum South* (New York: Pantheon, 1974), pp. 371–80.

3. Bureau of the Census, *Negro Population, 1790–1915* (Washington, D.C., 1918), pp. 90–92.

4. For the urban South see Rabinowitz, *Race Relations in the Urban South*; John W. Blassingame, *Black New Orleans, 1860–1880* (Chicago: University of Chicago Press, 1973); Robert E. Perdue, *The Negro in Savannah, 1865–1900* (New York: Exposition Press, 1973); Zane L. Miller, "Urban Blacks in the South, 1865–1920: An Analysis of Some Quantitative Data on Richmond, Savannah, New Orleans, Louisville, and Birmingham," in Leo F. Schnore, ed., *The New Urban History: Quantitative Explorations by American Historians* (Princeton: Princeton University Press, 1974), pp. 184–204; Robert Francis Engs, *Freedom's First Generation: Black Hampton, Virginia, 1861–1890* (Philadelphia: University of Pennsylvania Press, 1980); James Borchert, *Alley Life in Washington: Family, Community, Religion, and Folklife in the City, 1850–1970* (Urbana: University of Illinois Press, 1980); for the urban North see Gilbert Osofsky, *Harlem, the Making of a Ghetto: Negro New York, 1890–1930* (New York: Harper and Row, 1966); Allan H. Spear, *Black Chicago: The Making of a Negro Ghetto, 1890–1920* (Chicago: University of Chicago Press, 1969); David M. Katzman, *Before the Ghetto: Black Detroit in the Nineteenth Century* (Urbana: University of Illinois Press, 1973); Kenneth L. Kusmer, *A Ghetto Takes Shape: Black*

Cleveland, 1870–1930 (Urbana: University of Illinois Press, 1976); Harold X. Connolly, *A Ghetto Grows in Brooklyn* (New York: New York University Press, 1977); Elizabeth Hafkin Pleck, *Black Migration and Poverty: Boston, 1865–1900* (New York: Academic Press, 1979).

5. *Weekly Progress*, 26 September 1867.

6. *Montgomery Daily Ledger*, 23 September 1865.

7. *Weekly Progress*, 7 February 1867.

8. Quoted, W. E. B. Du Bois, ed., *The Negro Artisan*, Atlanta University Publications, no. 7, ed. W. E. B. Du Bois (Atlanta: Atlanta University Press, 1902), pp. 136–37.

9. Testimony of James O'Hara, in U.S. Senate, Forty-sixth Congress, Second Session, *Report and Testimony of the Select Committee of the United States Senate to Investigate the Causes for the Removal of the Negroes from the Southern States to the Northern States* (Washington, D.C.: Government Printing Office, 1880), part 1, p. 57.

10. J. Morgan Kousser, *The Shaping of Southern Politics: Suffrage Restriction and the Establishment of the One-Party South, 1880–1910* (New Haven: Yale University Press, 1974), pp. 183–95 and passim; Helen G. Edmonds, *The Negro and Fusion Politics in North Carolina, 1894–1901* (Chapel Hill: University of North Carolina Press, 1951), pp. 179–83.

11. On black leadership elsewhere see Howard N. Rabinowitz, ed., *Southern Black Leaders of the Reconstruction Era* (Urbana: University of Illinois Press, 1982).

12. I want to thank Professor John Hope Franklin for permitting me to look at his files on North Carolina free blacks drawn from the 1860 census. A perusal of his records for sixteen counties in the Raleigh area produced two of the councilmen. A third, James Harris, is known from other sources to have been free. It is likely that an additional one or two were free, but the absence of more names in the 1860 census suggests that most of those whose antebellum status is listed as "not available" were indeed slaves.

13. For often inaccurate discussions of Raleigh and North Carolina blacks after 1890 see Dorothy A. Gay, "Crisis of Identity: The Negro Community in Raleigh, 1890–1900," *North Carolina Historical Review* 50 (April 1973): 121–39; Frenise A. Logan, *The Negro in North Carolina, 1876–1894* (Chapel Hill: University of North Carolina Press, 1964); Edmonds, *Negro and Fusion Politics*.

14. Katzman, *Before the Ghetto*, pp. 136, 160–61; Kusmer, *A Ghetto Takes Shape*, pp. 30, 92–93, 97; David A. Gerber, *Black Ohio*

and the Color Line, 1860–1915 (Urbana: University of Illinois Press, 1976), pp. 56–57, 131–33.

15. Bureau of the Census, *Negro Population*, pp. 90–91.

16. Gerber, *Black Ohio*, chapters 3, 7, 8; Spear, *Black Chicago*, pp. 6–7; Katzman, *Before the Ghetto*, chapter 3; Kusmer, *A Ghetto Takes Shape*, pp. 14–17 and chapter 3; Pleck, *Black Migration and Poverty*, p. 29; W. E. B. Du Bois, *The Philadelphia Negro: A Social Study* (Philadelphia: Published for the University of Pennsylvania, 1899), pp. 417–18; Osofsky, *Harlem*, pp. 36–37.

17. Gerber, *Black Ohio*, chapter 8; Katzman, *Before the Ghetto*, pp. 33–37, 175–201; Du Bois, *Philadelphia Negro*, pp. 368–83; Lawrence Grossman, *The Democratic Party and the Negro: Northern and National Politics, 1868–92* (Urbana: University of Illinois Press, 1976).

18. For differences in the percentage of female-headed households in selected northern and southern cities see Pleck, *Black Migration and Poverty*, pp. 183–84. For the greater opportunities in northern cities for blacks especially as factory workers and clerks, see Kusmer, *A Ghetto Takes Shape*, pp. 17–24; Gerber, *Black Ohio*, pp. 60–80; Pleck, *Black Migration and Poverty*, pp. 147–49.

19. Katzman, *Before the Ghetto*, pp. 126–29; Gerber, *Black Ohio*, pp. 80–92; Kusmer, *A Ghetto Takes Shape*, pp. 98–103; Spear, *Black Chicago*, pp. 54–70, 111.

20. Katzman, *Before the Ghetto*, chapter 2, especially, pp. 77–78; Spear, *Black Chicago*, p. 6; Connolly, *A Ghetto Grows in Brooklyn*, pp. 7–8, 21–22; Kusmer, *A Ghetto Takes Shape*, pp. 12–13, and chapter 2, especially, p. 47; Gerber, *Black Ohio*, pp. 114–16.

21. See the books by Katzman, Kusmer, Spear, Osofsky, Connolly, and Gerber already cited.

6. The Education of Black Physicians at Shaw University, 1882–1918

Todd L. Savitt

In the 1912 Leonard Medical School catalog, Charles F. Meserve, the institution's president, boasted: "As a proof of the wisdom of the policy and methods of the Leonard Medical School, it can be stated that its graduates rarely fail to win for themselves positions of influence and usefulness in the communities where they settle. They are not obliged to go to States where a license is not required in order to practice medicine."[1] Two years later, in 1914, having trained more than four hundred black physicians (see Table 6-1) in its thirty-two years on the Raleigh, North Carolina, campus of Shaw University, Leonard Medical School reduced its teaching commitment from a four-year to a two-year (basic science) curriculum. In 1918 Leonard closed its doors forever. This was not the only black medical school to open and then cease operations during the late nineteenth and early twentieth centuries (see Table 6-2). Of the eleven founded during this time period, all of which began with similar high hopes, only two—Howard and Meharry —endured beyond the early 1920s.

One might argue that these schools were not providing medical training equal to that offered at, for example, Johns Hopkins or Harvard. Some in the medical reform establishment of the time saw little value in schools that turned out lesser-trained physicians. Abraham Flexner's famous 1910 report on medical education in the United States spoke for those with such attitudes: "A well-taught negro sanitarian will be immensely useful; an essentially untrained negro wearing an M.D. degree is dangerous."[2]

But were these medical schools really so poor as to deserve the fate they suffered? Did external pressures contribute to their de-

Table 6-1. *Leonard Medical School Students*

Year	Number of Students	Number of Graduates
1881–82	7	—
1882–83	11	—
1883–84	12	—
1884–85	17	—
1885–86	26	6
1886–87	28	—
1887–88	36	5
1888–89	42	7
1889–90	53	6
1890–91	48	6
1891–92	62	8
1892–93	60	10
1893–94	57	7
1894–95	56	8
1895–96	47	10
1896–97	51	7
1897–98	64	10
1898–99	78	4
1899–1900	80	13
1900–1901	98	18
1901–2	106	21
1902–3	113	14
1903–4	125	21
1904–5	136	21
1905–6	146	33
1906–7	149	24
1907–8	125	43
1908–9	—	22
1909–10	—	23
1910–11	128	22
1911–12	121	30
1912–13	104	—
1913–14	72	—

Table 6-2. *Black Medical Colleges, 1865–1920*

Name	City	Year Organized	Year Discontinued
Howard University	Washington, D.C.	1869	
Lincoln University	Oxford, Pa.	1870	1872
Meharry Medical College	Nashville, Tenn.	1876	
Leonard Medical School	Raleigh, N.C.	1882	1918
Louisville National Medical College	Louisville, Ky.	1888	1912
Flint Medical College	New Orleans, La.	1889	1911
Knoxville College Medical Dept.	Knoxville, Tenn.	1895	1900
Chattanooga National Medical College	Chattanooga, Tenn.	1899	1908
State University Medical Dept.	Louisville, Ky.	1899	1903
Knoxville Medical College	Knoxville, Tenn.	1900	1910
University of West Tennessee School of Medicine and	Jackson, Tenn.	1900	1907
Surgery	Memphis, Tenn.	1907	1923

mise? Judgments of quality aside, did these black medical schools provide for needs in the black population of the United States that would not have been met otherwise? The answers are important because after 1923 and the closing of those allegedly inferior black medical schools, only two institutions remained to train the vast majority of Negro physicians in the United States. The small number of black doctors during these past sixty years can be attributed in part to the closing of schools like Flint and Leonard.

Information adequate to answer questions about black medical education is difficult to obtain. Though the American Medical Association (AMA) published annual education and state licensure exam reports, neither the AMA nor the Association of American Medical Colleges (AAMC) preserved many original papers, letters, unpublished reports, or minutes of meetings of the late nineteenth century. Some important information was exchanged among leaders in medical education at the Carnegie

Foundation for the Advancement of Teaching (a cosponsor of the Flexner Report) and the General Education Board (a philanthropic wing of the Rockefeller family fortune that donated large sums to medical education). Those papers have been preserved. But, with one notable exception, records of black medical schools are scarce. Tucked off in a corner room of the Shaw University Library in Raleigh is a small archives that contains invaluable material on some of the operations of Leonard Medical School. On the Colgate-Rochester Divinity School campus in Rochester, New York, is another small cache of papers on Leonard—part of the American Baptist Historical Society collections. From these documents we can reconstruct a history of Leonard. The problems it encountered in its attempt to provide quality medical education to a generally poor, undereducated racial minority in the late nineteenth- and early twentieth-century South were typical of all such schools. Though the details were, of course, different for each school, the basic problems were similar. Thus, Leonard can serve as a case study for black medical education in general.

The seeds of failure at Leonard were sown early. Internal problems grew unchecked, making it increasingly difficult to respond to external pressures of the medical reform era. The school never had a chance to be self-sustaining. It could have been saved and improved, but no one was willing to take the necessary steps at any time in its thirty-six-year history.

Leonard Medical School was an addition to Shaw University, one of many institutions of higher learning established by Northerners for freedmen following the Civil War.[3] The New York–based American Baptist Home Mission Society (ABHMS), an organization with a long tradition of benevolence and missionary zeal, sponsored and supported Shaw in Raleigh as it grew from a small struggling school for local freedmen in 1865 to one of the larger and more highly regarded colleges for blacks at the turn of the century. During the period from 1865 to 1920 Shaw offered college preparatory, college-level, and theological courses, as well as, for various lengths of time, legal, pharmaceutical, medical, and missionary training programs.[4] With fateful significance Shaw was maintained as a charity institution, part of the larger

Fig. 6-1. Henry M. Tupper, a Massachusetts minister, engaged in missionary work in Raleigh under the auspices of the American Baptist Home Mission Society. In 1865 he established Raleigh Institute, later renamed Shaw University, and served as its first president. From Henry L. Morehouse, *H. M. Tupper: A Narrative of Twenty-five Years' Work in the South, 1865–90* (Baltimore, Md.: R. H. Woodward and Company, 1889), frontispiece.

mission of northern Baptists to aid and educate former slaves and their children and grandchildren. Funds came from the outside, for the most part, not from student fees, endowment funds, or local support—a weak system of funding that would plague the institution for much of its history.

The medical school at Shaw had its origins in the dreams of Henry M. Tupper (1811–93), the university's founder and first president. White and a native of Massachusetts, Tupper joined the Army of the Potomac shortly after graduating from Newton Theological Seminary in 1862. Deeply interested in serving the religious needs of blacks, the young minister decided, upon the cessation of hostilities, to do missionary work among the freedmen in Raleigh, North Carolina, under the auspices of the ABHMS. Tupper worked with small groups of blacks and during the second half of 1865 established a "theological class" that became the basis of a school.[5] Relying on contacts developed with the Freedmen's Bureau, ABHMS, and Baptists in Massachusetts, Tupper gained enough financial and salary support to establish a permanent school for the education of future black ministers. In 1870, Elijah Shaw, a woolen manufacturer of Wales, Massachusetts, donated five thousand dollars to aid in the purchase of land for a permanent home for the "Raleigh Institute." For this gift (and later ones) the school was renamed in his honor.[6]

According to Henry L. Morehouse, an officer of the ABHMS and well-known champion of black education during the late nineteenth century, Tupper had decided as early as 1866 to add a medical school at Shaw University when feasible.[7] The president explained this desire in Shaw catalogs during the 1870s: "The colored people at present are without educated Physicians, and thus are subject to all manner of quackery and imposition, and many suffer and die for want of medical attention."[8] Though the need was there, the wherewithal to undertake so ambitious an enterprise was not. Howard University had started its medical school in 1869 with, in part, federal financial support.[9] Central Tennessee College had just opened its medical department under the auspices of private philanthropists (the Meharry brothers) and the Freedmen's Aid Society of the Methodist Episcopal church.[10] Tupper had broached the subject of a medical school at Shaw

Fig. 6-2. Judson Wade Leonard, whose financial assistance to Shaw University permitted the construction of the Medical Dormitory. For this and other contributions, the medical school was named in his honor. Photograph courtesy of Shaw University, Raleigh.

several times with the ABHMS board and with wealthy, public-spirited Northerners, but as of 1878 had received only words of encouragement.[11] He reported great interest and enthusiasm among his students for the opening of a medical school.[12]

So anxious was the president to see this project through that he made a proposal to the ABHMS board that would later undermine the maintenance of the institution. At the time, however, the idea seemed logical, applicable, and feasible. Tupper's communication to the board read:

1st. I offer to purchase a site for building said department.

2nd. I will deliver the brick on the ground free of expense for said building, the building to be about 40 x 60 feet, three stories high.

3rd. I estimate that it will cost about $5,000 to erect the building and furnish it.

4th. I propose to find five men who will give $1,000 each, and think I can do it with the blessing of the Lord.

5th. Form a class next October, and have the building completed one year from next October.

6th. Make the tuition pay for the medical instruction.

7th. If there be objections to having the Home Mission Society engage in such a department of work, let the trustees operate this department of the school independent of the Home Mission Society. Why not? We are all brethren.

8th. There is no medical college for colored people from Washington to New Orleans.[13]

He managed to gain the board's official, conditional, but still only spiritual endorsement in December 1878.[14] Tupper then quickly took action.

He did not find five $1,000 donors; rather he came up with one, his brother-in-law, Judson Wade Leonard of Hampden, Massachusetts, who pledged the whole $5,000 on condition that a matching amount be raised within six months.[15] The Home Mission Board endorsed Leonard's philanthropy and encouraged others to follow suit by publicizing the gift in its new magazine, the *Baptist Home Mission Monthly*.[16] To raise remaining funds, Tup-

Fig. 6-3. Medical Dormitory, Shaw University. This thirty-four-room medical dormitory was completed in the spring of 1881. From *Biennial Report of the Superintendent of Public Instruction of North Carolina for the Years 1896–97 and 1897–98* (Raleigh: Guy V. Barnes, 1898), facing p. 610.

per traveled north after the spring 1880 school term. He returned to Raleigh in July with $3,900 in cash and pledges, enough to feel confident about further pursuit of his proposal.[17]

Shaw students had actually been engaged in digging clay for brickmaking since January 1880.[18] Now the work began in earnest.[19] The thirty-four-room medical dormitory was completed in the spring of 1881.[20] While the dormitory was under construction, Tupper turned his energies to securing land for a medical classroom and laboratory building. An appeal to the North Carolina General Assembly netted Shaw a square acre of land adjacent to the campus—land that had been part of the governor's mansion lot. The legislature designated this plot specifically for Shaw's medical school.[21] Spurred by this success in March 1881, Tupper turned again to his wife's brother to fund the medical science building. And again Leonard came through. By the fall of 1882 Leonard Medical School had two new buildings and some extra

Fig. 6-4. Leonard Medical School, Shaw University. This building, adjacent to the campus, was constructed in 1882 on an acre of land that the North Carolina legislature designated for Shaw's medical school. From *Biennial Report of the Superintendent of Public Instruction of North Carolina for the Years 1896–97 and 1897–98* (Raleigh: Guy V. Barnes, 1898), facing p. 674.

land.[22] Tupper then secured the services of "some of the leading white physicians of Raleigh" to teach at the school and obtained partial support from drug manufacturers for establishment of a dispensary so "that our medical students may have the advantages of clinical instruction."[23] During the previous year thirteen students had pursued a preliminary medical course in anticipation of matriculation at Leonard. Tupper was pleased with the school's progress. The only hint of future problems was this brief allusion in an enthusiastic report to *Baptist Home Mission Monthly* readers in the summer of 1882: "If we have the ability to furnish our medical building with apparatus and appliances, so as to make it a first-class medical school, we may expect to see it crowded with students."[24]

That was a big "if," especially in view of the sixth and seventh items in Tupper's proposal to the ABHMS board. According to

Fig. 6-5. Leonard Pharmacy, Shaw University. President Henry M. Tupper secured support from drug manufacturers for the establishment of a dispensary. Photograph courtesy of Shaw University, Raleigh.

these sections, he intended to have tuition fees cover the cost of medical instruction. The Leonard Medical School was to be self-sufficient—not a drain on Shaw's other programs or on the university's main financial support, the ABHMS. The ABHMS board, in fact, had emphasized from the outset that though it approved of Leonard, it also had no financial obligations to the school.[25] Here, then, was the root of Leonard's biggest problem and the cause of its ultimate failure—money. The problem existed from the school's inception. Tuition fees never paid the medical instruction expenses. The Leonard family's gifts really amounted only to the funding of two buildings, establishment of a small ($5,000) scholarship fund, and occasional small donations to cover shortfalls in operating expenses. A few donations from the Rockefeller family over the years helped ease specific financial problems.[26] But no substantial endowment fund existed. No other northern philanthropists and no wealthy graduates of the medical school gave large sums to Leonard Medical School. The state offered no further assistance. Leonard, in fact, soon became a financial drain on Shaw, precisely the situation Tupper and the ABHMS board had sought to avoid. Leonard could not become the first-class institution Tupper had dreamed about until it obtained proper funding. That never happened.

Tupper, of course, understood Leonard's financial needs, but could not have predicted their persistence in November 1882, when the first class of students formally began its studies. He simply proceeded according to plan. The catalog published for 1881–82 listed eight students in the preliminary course and seven in the regular recitation course (though two students were listed in both).[27] The following academic year (1882–83), during which the medical school had its official opening, three young men matriculated as second-year students and eight as first-year. At the end of that school term, Tupper expressed satisfaction, pronounced the school "a grand success," and praised the students in nineteenth-century white paternalistic terms. "In the medical department, the closing examination was very satisfactory indeed. The students have studied with diligence and more enthusiasm than I have ever witnessed among colored students, and those competent to judge, do not hesitate to give as their opinion, that the class has made as much progress as is usually done by white students. Our medical school is a grand success."[28]

Leonard soon received national recognition from two different sources. First, the newly created John F. Slater Fund, established by a Massachusetts businessman to assist in the education of worthy black students, donated five hundred dollars to Leonard Medical School, half for purchase of medical apparatus, half for student scholarships. Though the amount fluctuated, Slater Fund money aided Leonard Medical School annually until 1905.[29] Second, *Medical News*, a prestigious Philadelphia medical journal, included a one-column notice of the school based on information contained in the college catalog and Shaw's student newspaper, the *African Expositor*. The story, written by one of Shaw's trustees, Dr. W. W. Keen, extended a warm welcome to Leonard Medical School and a wish for its success. "[Blacks] need physicians of their own race, and this medical school will not only provide them, but will also open a new avenue of self-support to the black man."[30]

Ironically, Leonard received a very different sort of greeting from home-state physicians. Noting that his information derived from the *Medical News* article rather than directly from authorities at Leonard Medical School, Thomas F. Wood, editor of the *North Carolina Medical Journal* (Wilmington), remarked: "We have never seen any authoritative account of this Medical College, but we trust that the good sense of the managers of it will prevail, and that they will allow it to cease, before much harm is done."[31] Because, according to his information, the school offered shorter terms than other schools and only a three-year curriculum, Wood felt Leonard Medical School graduates would be less well trained than their white counterparts. "In fact a much larger course should be prescribed for them, as they have more difficulties to overcome." Blacks, he continued, lacked the "degree of inborn quickness of perception of which the higher races are remarkable, and superadded to this a long training of the senses, and an immense amount of learning is necessary for success in the medical profession."[32] The editor then jabbed at the smallness of Raleigh, the quality of Leonard Medical School's teaching staff (three white Raleigh physicians), and the poor learning capability blacks had displayed in other educational situations. He predicted the failure of the medical school.[33]

Though black students did have some educational deficiencies owing to poor basic schooling and the constant pressures of poverty, Tupper remained undaunted. At first, he later recalled, "there were few who had pursued their [preliminary] studies a sufficient length of time to commence that of medicine, and it took two years—from 1880 to 1882—to find half a dozen in all our schools who were competent to enter our Medical Department."[34] That problem seemed to have been overcome by the 1885–86 session (see Table 6-1). Once embarked on the new medical course, Tupper, his white medical faculty, and his black medical students strove for success.

Thanks to the generosity of northern friends of Shaw University, the lecture rooms and laboratories were soon stocked with supplies and anatomy models.[35] In January 1885 the twenty-five-bed Leonard Hospital opened its doors to the sick and poor of the local black community and to the medical students of Leonard.

Fig. 6-6. First Leonard Medical School class. Leonard's 1885–86 enrollment was twenty-six. Graduates of the first class, 1886, were M. S. G. Abbott, James H. Bugg, M. T. Pope, A. T. Prince, and L. A. Scruggs. Photograph courtesy of Shaw University, Raleigh.

Clinical instruction, increasingly recognized as an essential component of good medical education, was now provided. (Unfortunately for patients and students, for those months when school was out of session, the hospital closed.) Again, as with all other aspects of Leonard Medical School's development, private northern philanthropy and local black fund raising through fairs and community appeals financed the school's programs. The ABHMS allocated no money.[36]

When, in 1886, the first six students had completed their studies and exams and were ready for graduation, Shaw University celebrated. The Reverend Mr. Tupper wrote in the *African Expositor*, the school's newspaper: "Few events connected with the founding of Shaw University have ever awakened so deep an interest as the closing exercises of the Leonard Medical School, on the evening of March 31st."[37] In addition to students and invited guests, a large number of interested black citizens attended the ceremonies. Eugene Grissom, M.D., superintendent of the North Carolina Insane Asylum in Raleigh (later called Doro-

Fig. 6-7. Lawson Andrew Scruggs, valedictorian, class of 1886, practiced medicine in Raleigh and assumed teaching responsibilities at Leonard Medical School. From Lawson Andrew Scruggs, *Women of Distinction: Remarkable in Works and Invincible in Character* (Raleigh: L. A. Scruggs, 1893), frontispiece.

thea Dix Hospital), who delivered the keynote address, treated the occasion with the same seriousness and earnestness he would have given a white medical school graduation. Not once did he allude to the uniqueness of this commencement or to the race of the young physicians being honored.[38] It was L. A. Scruggs of Liberty, Virginia, the class valedictorian and soon-to-be resident physician at Leonard Hospital, who brought home that message to an audience that did not really need reminding. "The colored man must go forward," he announced in an oration entitled "Medical Education as a Factor in the Elevation of the Colored Race." "He must harness himself for the battle, and we who stand before you tonight, are pioneers of the medical profession of our race." He concluded with the hope that black physicians would increase rapidly in number and so improve Negro health, both at home and in Africa, and that the race would then be in a position to concern itself with spiritual, moral, and economic elevation.[39]

Demonstrating the capabilities of blacks as physicians, Leonard's first graduates succeeded admirably on the state licensure exams. Tupper reported gleefully in 1886 to the school's trustees and to the ABHMS: "The best evidence that the school is doing good work is the fact that those who graduated at the close of last session and recently presented themselves before the State Medical Board passed a creditable examination, much to the surprise of some of the examiners. The scene as described by one of our faculty, also a member of the State Medical Board, was, to say the least, intensely interesting and exceedingly gratifying."[40] During Tupper's remaining seven years as president of Shaw, students who graduated continued to perform well on state boards.[41] Meanwhile, regular Leonard Medical School budgetary deficits seemed to disappear with the annual emergency financial help of northern friends, medical faculty teaching by local physicians remained stable and satisfactory,[42] and new black doctors found good locations for their practices.[43] Leonard Medical School was, to all outward appearances, succeeding.

On 12 November 1893 Shaw University and Leonard Medical School marked the end of an era: the Reverend Henry M. Tupper died after twenty-eight years of service to the institution he had founded. To succeed him the ABHMS and the university's trust-

Fig. 6-8. Charles F. Meserve succeeded Henry M. Tupper as president of Shaw University in 1894. Under his presidency Leonard's four-year medical curriculum became a two-year basic science curriculum in 1914; it ceased operations four years later. Photograph from files of the North Carolina Division of Archives and History, Raleigh.

ees selected Charles Francis Meserve, a forty-four-year-old New Englander with twelve years' experience as superintendent of Haskell Institute, a large Indian industrial training school in Lawrence, Kansas.[44]

Meserve found financial matters at Shaw in an alarming state when he arrived in Raleigh in March 1894. He wrote in his 1894 *Annual Report*:

I found the departments of Law, Medicine and Pharmacy
in good condition, but it is these three departments that
have caused the financial strain through which the University is passing. . . . I am not prepared to recommend the
discontinuance of these departments for the reason that they
are of such high order and have done such grand work. . . .
It is, however, but true to state that these departments
cannot continue unless money is forthcoming from some
source.[45]

Meserve thus put the school's trustees and the ABHMS on
notice that he would not jeopardize Shaw's existence for the sake
of the medical, law, and pharmacy schools. It was not that he
opposed training black professionals. On the contrary, in an inter-
view Meserve granted a Raleigh *News and Observer* reporter in
September 1895, the president stated: "The colored people need
those of their own race in the professions. . . . Why, now, we
can't begin to supply the demand for physicians. Not long ago, I
had a letter from the private secretary of the Governor of Alabama, asking us to send them physicians, there was a county
containing 22,000 colored people, with no physician among them
of their own race."[46] For Meserve, though, Leonard was but part
of a greater enterprise, Shaw University. When he acted to close
the medical school some twenty years later, he did so to save that
larger enterprise.

The institution's financial instability was, of course, an old
story. As early as 1886, the year of Leonard's first graduation,
the need for a large endowment fund had been recognized. Using
the *African Expositor* and the *Baptist Home Mission Monthly*,
Tupper at that time made regular appeals to northern Baptists for
$40,000 or $50,000 and, when that amount was not forthcoming,
for $25,000. In an 1886 article entitled "The Leonard Medical
School, Shaw University—Its Endowment a Necessity," Tupper
further explained that the $5,000 endowment fund Leonard then
possessed yielded only about $250 per annum, which, combined
with the low tuition of $60 per student, barely paid operating
expenses such as fuel, repairs, and regular additions to the teaching equipment. Salaries for the instructors alone totaled $2,750,

an amount difficult to raise each year. These regular appeals for money from northern friends consumed much of Tupper's time and energy. "We are sure," he continued, "a moment of reflection will convince any one that the present financial condition of our Medical Department must be a source of anxiety, if not of wasted energies."[47] By the spring of 1888, two graduations later, the situation had not changed. For the previous six months the *Baptist Home Mission Monthly* had advertised for "a $25,000 Christian philanthropist," but to no avail.[48] Still, Tupper and the ABHMS "earnestly hoped for" his appearance.[49] An expanded version of Dr. Scruggs's valedictory address on black medical education was published in the Christmas 1888 issue of the *Monthly* in hopes of stimulating interest, but again with no success.[50]

Other southern black schools found themselves facing similar situations. By the late 1880s and 1890s the strong sense of mission that had stimulated and sustained northern interest in the welfare of former slaves was waning. The very term "freedman" now seemed anachronistic. Though missionary organizations like the ABHMS continued to provide evidence of southern blacks' educational needs, northern benefactors seemed to be losing the paternalistic spirit that had existed twenty-five and thirty years earlier. Black migration to northern towns and new interests in caring for the large numbers of European immigrants in the northern United States also contributed to a declining concern for southern blacks. Furthermore, money had become tighter during the economic turmoil of the 1890s. Not surprisingly, then, ABHMS field secretary Henry L. Morehouse wrote a long article for the *Monthly* in 1894 proclaiming "a great crisis in our educational work for the colored people and the Indians." The ABHMS could not, he maintained, support with present funds all the educational activities for which it was responsible without curtailing its other, equally important missionary work. In explaining the need for a permanent endowment to relieve this crisis, Morehouse pointed to the severe distresses at Shaw. "Even now, the very existence of the excellent medical and industrial department of Shaw University is trembling in the balance for the lack of $6,000. Dr. Tupper's death takes away the skillful management which has kept those departments in successful operation. They are not and cannot be maintained by the Society, both for lack of means and because this is not its legitimate work."[51] It was at this inauspicious moment in Leonard's financial history that Meserve assumed the presidency of Shaw.

The situation was grim. Meserve discovered and reported to the Slater Fund agent in a carefully written but frank letter of appeal that for a few years before his death Tupper had borrowed "large sums of money at a high rate of interest to keep the institution alive." He described in detail Tupper's actions to save the medical school.

> My predecessor was enabled to keep the institution going only by devoting all the money he could possibly collect from the students and other sources to paying the salaries of the medical professors. Even this was not sufficient, for year by year he was obliged to transfer funds from other departments to the medical, and, after this was done there was a large deficiency which was met by borrowing from banks. This is not all paid yet. To such an extent was this carried on that he was not able to equip the medical school with the apparatus that is so indispensible in such an institution. Furthermore, the buildings in all departments have been neglected, and imperatively demanded repairs were not made, so that all the money possible from all departments might be saved and devoted to paying the salaries in the medical department. To such an extent was this carried on that some of the buildings were endangered, and there is not a building here but what needs extensive repairs both outside and inside in order to prevent decay and destruction.[52]

Not only was Leonard Medical School in danger of failing, but its problems were threatening Shaw as a whole.

For Meserve, nonreligious activities such as medical education were not the proper work of missionary associations such as the ABHMS. He felt strongly that Shaw should remain first and foremost a vehicle for teaching Baptist principles to blacks and for producing good, Christian teachers who would then spread their knowledge and faith to other blacks. As he explained it to the Slater Fund agent, "It would be impracticable for the Home Mission Society, organized distinctively for the prosecution of Missions and collecting its money from the churches for that purpose, to engage in the general work of educating Negroes of the South especially along the higher professional lines. . . . It does not feel warranted . . . in attempting to carry on a Medical School, a School of Pharmacy, and a Law School, to be paid for out of its Mission fund."[53]

Desperate to eliminate the primary drain on Leonard's fiscal resources, medical faculty salaries, Meserve explained the problem in full to J. L. M. Curry, agent for the Slater Fund, and asked for help. The $1,000 that Slater already gave annually paid the salaries of two teachers, both of whom received $100 per month for the five-month term. Meserve now asked Slater also to pick up the six remaining faculty salaries, totaling $2,750, "to save the life of the institution." He minced no words. "The closing of the medical school is staring us in the face on account of inability to meet running expenses." In addition to financial exigencies, Meserve argued, Shaw was a fitting recipient of Slater money because the funds would be used to pay an unusual faculty. "Its Faculty is unique, consisting of seven white Professors, men who were born and bred in the South and who are all practicing physicians in the City. . . . These white physicians [are] doing more to break down any prejudice that may have existed and to build up education for the colored people in the South, than could be done in any other way."[54] For reasons not spelled out in Slater Fund or other records, that organization refused to increase its allowance to Leonard, and, in fact, ten years later ceased funding the medical school entirely.[55]

Somehow, by dint of skimping and sacrificing on the part of faculty and students alike, Shaw and Leonard made it through the 1895 crisis. The old debts were paid off.[56] But again the basic problem had not been solved, only patched over. Leonard needed an endowment so that its instructors could be paid, its needy students funded with scholarships, its laboratories and classrooms regularly restocked with supplies, and its hospital enlarged and opened year-round. Leonard needed to grow with the times, but it could not.

Outside the walls of Leonard Medical School times were certainly changing for medicine. Louis Pasteur and Robert Koch had proven that microbes caused disease, ushering in the era of bacteriology. German scientists had moved medicine into the laboratory, from which they were reporting exciting developments in pathology, physiology, immunology, and microbiology. Innovative surgery was being performed. Students studying abroad brought these new techniques and ideas back to the United States, where standards of medical education began to improve. The opening of the Johns Hopkins Medical School in 1893 symbolized that improvement. Furthermore, some medical educators began to feel that the rapid, uncontrolled proliferation of proprietary medical schools, which had been occurring since the Civil War, had to be reversed. The Association of American Medical Colleges, the American Medical Association's Council on Medical Education, and the individual state boards of medical examiners all now strove to increase the standards of medical education.[57]

These events were beginning to occur just as Leonard Medical School was getting its start. As the AAMC gained more member schools and began setting the standards, and as state examining boards incorporated more and more new medical and basic scientific information into their tests, medical colleges like Leonard found themselves in trouble. Longer school terms, better-trained faculty members, improved clinical facilities, modern technological and chemical equipment, new laboratories, and solidly educated students were needed.

Failure rates on state licensure exams became the measure of a school's worth, once the American Medical Association began publishing this information in 1904. Leonard did not fare so well, either in comparison with other black schools or with other medical students around the country (see Figures 6-9 and 6-10). In the periodic inspections that the American Medical Association's Council on Medical Education made after 1904, Leonard always received C ratings, compared with Howard's and Meharry's A's and B's.[58] Flexner, in 1910, had little good to say. Of the laboratory facilities, for example, he reported: "These comprise a clean and exceedingly well kept dissecting-room, a slight chemical laboratory, and a still slighter equipment for pathology. There are no library, no museum, and no teaching accessories. It is

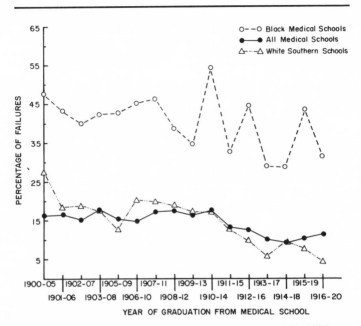

Fig. 6-9. Failure rate on state medical licensure exams, 1900–1920.

evident that the policy of paying practitioners [to teach] has absorbed the resources of a school that exists for purely philanthropic objects." The report added that clinical facilities were "normal," consisting of a sixteen-bed hospital with only three patients at the time of the visit, and "no dispensary [out-patient clinic] at all."[59] Flexner's comments underscored the problems facing Leonard.

Spurred on by these negative statements, the school's administration tried desperately to keep up. Terms were lengthened gradually from four to eight months, laboratories were upgraded and new ones built, microscopes were purchased, admissions standards were raised, more faculty and courses were added, and finally in 1911 a new, modern hospital was constructed.[60] But still, at the core, lack of money wore Leonard down. The local Raleigh doctors who made up the faculty did their best, but many

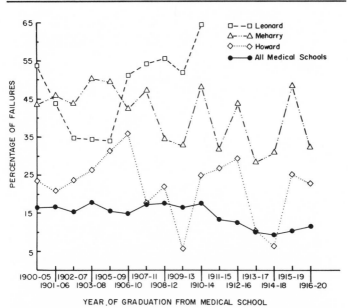

Fig. 6-10. Failure rate on state medical licensure exams for three black medical schools, 1900–1920.

had trained in the prebacteriology era with its different approach to medicine. They gave their time at no small cost. Leonard Medical School could not afford to bring in many of the new breed of scientific physicians or basic science teachers. The school was too far behind to catch up without a large infusion of money to upgrade faculty, students, and facilities. Despite Meserve's optimism in the 1912 catalog, Leonard was doomed. Rockefeller's General Education Board saw Meharry, a bigger, more dynamic black medical school in Nashville, and Howard, more visible in Washington, D.C., and possessing better facilities, as the logical recipients of its largess in the area of black medical education.[61] Leonard did not have the growth potential, the financial strength, or the strong faculty to meet the higher educational standards of a new era.

Table 6-3. *White and Black Physicians in United States Population*

	No. Black M.D.s	No. White M.D.s	Black M.D.s/ Black and White M.D.s (percentage)	White Pop. per White M.D.	Black Pop. per Black M.D.
1890	909	103,482	.87	533	8,238
1900	1,734	129,841	1.32	516	5,098
1910	3,077	147,741	2.04	553	3,194
1920	3,495	141,237	2.41	671	2,994
1930	3,805	149,527	2.48	728	3,125

Source: U.S. Censuses, 1890–1930.

Unquestionably, as Table 6-3 shows, more black doctors were needed, and General Education Board money could have been well spent at Leonard. Letters from Leonard graduates in practice indicated that they were faring well, seemingly as well as their counterparts from Howard and Meharry.[62] At the end of the 1914 term, however, Leonard Medical School closed the newly built Leonard Hospital and reduced its program to a two-year basic science curriculum. In 1918 Leonard Medical School closed its doors forever. The editors of the fledgling black-run *Journal of the National Medical Association* sadly but wholeheartedly agreed with the trustees' decision.

> Our . . . requiem for the school . . . is fare thee well Old Leonard, your work is done. Honor to you and to the lamented and beloved Dr. Henry M. Tupper who brought you into existence. Honor to those who fostered you and gave you support. Honor to your noble professors. Honor to the many sons whom you sent into the world who are today the only living vestige of your having existed. We love you, Old Leonard, and mourn your loss, but we recognize that this is a new era, a new day has dawned—your work is done. . . . All standards of education, and especially medical education, have been raised. . . . Not being able to meet these exacting conditions, it was necessary that you

die, and while it is with great sorrow, we had far rather bid
thee farewell than to have you merely to exist.[63]

Leonard closed because of underfinancing, because no individual or organization was ever willing to step in and support it
monetarily. By 1910, when Flexner wrote his negative report,
even the promise of a new clinical facility (the expanded Leonard
Hospital) could not alter the school's pattern of decline. Leonard
needed an endowment and operating capital to pay professors,
buy equipment, maintain teaching and clinical laboratories, and
provide for the other usual expenses of a modern medical school.
Instead the school drew off funds from the rest of the university,
impeding, indeed reversing, the growth of the larger institution.
Meserve had to close Leonard to save Shaw. He could hang on no
longer. So, having satisfied a need for some thirty-six years,
Leonard Medical School passed quietly from existence.

NOTES

This publication was supported in part by National Institutes of Health
Grant LM 03413 and by University of Florida Seed Money and
Biomedical Research grants. Thanks are extended to Mr. Clarence
Toomer, Ms. Robena Bradley, and the staff at the Shaw University Li-
brary for their assistance in locating and using early records of the
school.

1. *Annual Catalog of the Officers and Students of the Leonard Medical School . . . for the Academic Year Ending May Thirty-first Nineteen
Hundred and Twelve*, p. 9, Shaw University Archives, Raleigh, N.C.
Hereafter Leonard Medical (or Shaw University) catalogs will be cited
as *Leonard* (or *Shaw*) *Catalog*, followed by academic year and page
number. Broken runs of these catalogs may be found at the National Library of Medicine, Bethesda, Md., and the American Baptist Historical
Society Archives, Rochester, N.Y.

2. Abraham Flexner, *Medical Education in the United States and
Canada: A Report to the Carnegie Foundation for the Advancement of
Teaching* (Boston: Merrymount Press, 1910), p. 180.

3. For background on this subject see Henry Allen Bullock, *A History of Negro Education in the South from 1619 to the Present* (New
York: Praeger, 1967).

4. For a comprehensive history of Shaw University see Wilmoth A. Carter, *Shaw's Universe: A Monument to Educational Innovation* (Washington, D.C.: D.C. National Publishing, 1972).

5. Henry L. Morehouse, *A Narrative of Twenty-Five Years' Work in the South, 1865–1890* (New York: American Baptist Home Mission Society, [1890]), p. 8.

6. Ibid., pp. 5–10; Carter, *Shaw's Universe*, pp. 1–9.

7. Morehouse, *Narrative*, p. 13.

8. *Shaw Catalog, 1876–77*, p. 18; *1877–78*, p. 19; *1878–79*, p. 18; *1879–80*, p. 18.

9. Walter Dyson, *Howard University, the Capstone of Negro Education: A History, 1867–1940* (Washington, D.C.: Howard University, 1941), pp. 301–34. Herbert M. Morais, *The History of the Afro-American in Medicine* (Cornwell's Heights, Pa.: Publishers Agency, 1976), pp. 42–43.

10. Bullock, *History of Negro Education*, p. 33; Morais, *Afro-American in Medicine*, p. 44.

11. *Shaw Catalog, 1876–77*, pp. 18–19; *1877–78*, p. 19; *1878–79*, p. 18. The quotation appears in each catalog.

12. See footnote 11.

13. Henry M. Tupper to Dr. S. S. Cutting [Corresponding Secretary of the ABHMS], ca. December 1878, in Charles F. Meserve, "A History of Shaw University, Raleigh, North Carolina, 1865–1930," unpublished typescript at American Baptist Historical Society, Rochester, N.Y., unpaginated.

14. *Shaw Catalog, 1878–79*, p. 18.

15. Ibid.; *1879–80*, p. 18. *Baptist Home Mission Monthly* 2 (1880): 35.

16. *Baptist Home Mission Monthly* 2 (1880): 105.

17. Ibid., p. 155.

18. Ibid., p. 35.

19. Ibid., p. 155.

20. Ibid., 2 (1880): 219, 3 (1881): 15; Meserve, "History of Shaw."

21. *Laws of North Carolina, 1881*, c. 149; Carter, *Shaw's Universe*, pp. 27–28.

22. Meserve, "History of Shaw"; *Baptist Home Mission Monthly* 3 (1881): 191, 4 (1882): 216.

23. *Baptist Home Mission Monthly* 4 (1882): 216.

24. Ibid.

25. *Baptist Home Mission Monthly* 2 (1880): 105.

26. American Baptist Home Mission Society Executive Board Min-

utes, 11 June 1883, book 9, p. 438, at American Baptist Historical Society, Rochester, N.Y.; Shaw University Trustees Minutes, 30 April 1903 and 4 February 1910, in Shaw University Archives.

27. *Shaw Catalog, 1881–82*, p. 22.

28. *Baptist Home Mission Monthly* 5 (1883): 101.

29. *President's Annual Report to the Board of Trustees of Shaw University and to the Secretary of the American Baptist Home Mission Society* [December 1883], p. 6, Shaw University Archives (hereafter cited as *Shaw Annual Report*). See also John F. Slater Fund *Annual Reports* for these years; these are published and available in most university research libraries.

30. *Medical News* 43 (1883): 76.

31. *North Carolina Medical Journal* 12 (1883): 220.

32. Ibid. Leonard was one of the first (if not *the* first) medical schools to inaugurate a four-year graded curriculum. See *Leonard Medical School Announcement for the Session 1885–86*, p. 9, Shaw University Archives.

33. *North Carolina Medical Journal* 12 (1883): 221.

34. *Baptist Home Mission Monthly* 14 (1892): 271.

35. Ibid., 5 (1883): 196; Raleigh *Farmer and Mechanic*, 30 January 1884; *Leonard Announcement for 1885–86*, p. 8.

36. *Leonard Announcement for 1885–86*, p. 8; *Shaw Annual Report, 1885*, p. 6.

37. *African Expositor* (April 1886), North Carolina Collection, Wilson Library, University of North Carolina at Chapel Hill.

38. Ibid., pp. 2, 4.

39. Ibid., p. 3.

40. *Shaw Annual Report, 1886*, p. 3. See also *Baptist Home Mission Monthly* 8 (1886): 146.

41. *Shaw Annual Report, 1888*, p. 3; *1889*, p. 2; *1891*, p. 4; *1893*, p. 3. *Baptist Home Mission Monthly* 15 (1893): 254–55.

42. *Shaw Annual Reports, 1887–1893*, passim.

43. *Baptist Home Mission Monthly* 9 (1887): 64.

44. Ibid., 16 (1894): 2.

45. *Shaw Annual Report, 1894*, p. 3.

46. Raleigh *News and Observer*, 29 September 1895.

47. *Baptist Home Mission Monthly* 8 (1886): 56.

48. Ibid., 10 (1888): 125.

49. Ibid., p. 219.

50. Ibid., pp. 333, 350–53.

51. Ibid., 16 (1894): 103. This change in attitude and missionary pri-

orities is well demonstrated in the pages of the *Baptist Home Mission Monthly* for that period.

52. C. F. Meserve to J. L. M. Curry, 9 January 1895, in Meserve Letter Book, p. 43., Shaw University Archives.

53. Ibid., p. 46.

54. Ibid., p. 45.

55. See Slater Fund *Annual Reports* for these years.

56. C. F. Meserve to General T. J. Morgan, 23 March 1895, in C. F. Meserve Letter Book, p. 317; *Shaw Annual Report, 1895*, pp. 3–6.

57. For background information on medical education see Martin Kaufman, *American Medical Education: The Formative Years, 1765–1920* (Westport, Conn.: Greenwood Press, 1976); Robert P. Hudson, "Abraham Flexner in Perspective: American Medical Education, 1865–1910," *Bulletin of the History of Medicine* 56 (Nov.–Dec. 1972): 545–61.

58. See annual education issues of *Journal of the American Medical Association* for those years.

59. Flexner, *Medical Education in the United States*, pp. 280–81.

60. See *Leonard Catalogs* for these years.

61. E. Richard Brown, *Rockefeller Medicine Men: Medicine and Capitalism in America* (Berkeley and Los Angeles: University of California Press, 1979), pp. 153, 165–66.

62. See, for instance, William A. Mapp, M.D., to C. F. Meserve, 30 December 1896; J. H. G. Williams, M.D., to same, 12 May 1904; B. F. Hutchins, M.D., to same, 26 April 1904, all in Letters Received Files, Shaw University Archives.

63. *Journal of the National Medical Association* 10 (1918): 126.

Contributors

Lorin Lee Cary, a professor of history at the University of Toledo, teaches labor history. In addition to his studies of slavery in colonial North Carolina with Marvin L. Michael Kay, he has written a number of articles on different aspects of the American working class and, with Ray Boryczka, an illustrated book about workers in Ohio between 1803 and 1980. At present he is studying labor organizers between 1880 and 1980 and the black community of Nantucket, Massachusetts, 1700–1865.

Leland Ferguson is associate professor of anthropology at the University of South Carolina. He has conducted research and written articles on the anthropological history of all three of the major ethnic groups of the southeastern United States. Specializing in the technique of historical archaeology, he has promoted an integration of written history, folklore, and archaeology for the study of the American people. He was editor of and a contributor to *Historical Archaeology and the Importance of Material Things* (Society for Historical Archaeology, 1976)—a volume dedicated to developing the role of material studies in an integrated historical science.

Raymond Gavins holds a Ph.D. degree from the University of Virginia and is associate professor, specializing in Afro-American and southern history, at Duke University. In addition to articles and chapters on biography, migration, and segregation, he is author of *The Perils and Prospects of Southern Black Leadership: Gordon Blaine Hancock, 1884–1970* (Durham, 1977). Currently writing a one-volume study of the Negro in North Carolina, he is especially interested in the black South's institutional and intellectual development during the half-century before the *Brown* decision of 1954.

Marvin L. Michael Kay is a professor of history at the University of Toledo. He is the author of numerous articles on colonial North Carolina, some of which have been written with either Lorin Lee Cary or William S. Price, Jr. Recently, he has completed a book with Cary on slavery in colonial North Carolina. Currently, he is completing work on a monograph and book on the North Carolina Regulators and a series of computer analyses with Karl Vezner, Department of Political Science, University of Toledo. The work with Vezner attempts to assess the impact of the American Revolution upon North Carolina, particularly in the areas of wealth distribution, mobility, class, and ideology.

Linda M. Perkins, formerly the assistant director of the Mary Ingraham Bunting Institute of Radcliffe College, is now the assistant vice-president of the Claremont University Center, Claremont, California. She holds a Ph.D. from the University of Illinois, Champaign-Urbana, in the history of education and higher education. Her research is focused on nineteenth-century black educational history and particularly the educational activities of black women. Besides numerous articles in scholarly journals, she has written "The Nineteenth-Century Black Woman and Racial 'Uplift' prior to Emancipation" in Filomena Steady, ed., *The Black Woman: Cross Culturally* (Cambridge, 1981), and "Quaker Beneficence and Black Control: The Institute for Colored Youth, 1852–1903" in Vincent P. Franklin and James D. Anderson, eds., *New Perspectives on Black Educational History* (Boston, 1978). She is currently completing a book on nineteenth-century black women educators.

Howard N. Rabinowitz received his Ph.D. from the University of Chicago in 1973 and is currently associate professor of history at the University of New Mexico. He is the author of *Race Relations in the Urban South* (New York, 1978) and the editor of and a contributor to *Southern Black Leaders of the Reconstruction Era* (Urbana, 1982). His articles have appeared in the *Journal of American History*, *Journal of Southern History*, and other journals and in several anthologies that include *The City in Southern History* (New York, 1977) and *Ordinary People and Everyday Life: Perspectives on the New Social History* (Nashville, 1983). Among his current projects is a history of the South from 1877 to 1920.

Todd L. Savitt is associate professor of humanities in the School of Medicine and associate professor of history at East Carolina University. He received his Ph.D. in American history at the University of Virginia in 1975 and studied history of medicine and science at Duke University from 1974 to 1976. He taught history and (medical) humanities at the University of Florida from 1976 to 1982. His research focuses on black health in the United States. He is the author of *Medicine and Slavery* (Urbana, 1978) and the forthcoming *Physicians for Freedmen: Black Medical Education, 1865–1920*.

Index